The Real Cost of Regeneration

Judgment and the Limits of Modern Organizations

Written by Joel Carboni

For Syimah

Copyright © 2026 by Joel Carboni

First edition

ISBN: 979-8-218-93541-2

Printed in the United States of America

Joelcarboni.com

About the Author

Dr. Joel Carboni is a writer, practitioner, and systems thinker whose work focuses on how organizations translate intention into consequence. For more than two decades, he has worked at the intersection of leadership, governance, and sustainability, advising boards, executives, and institutions on why well-intentioned decisions so often produce harm that no one appears to have chosen.

He is best known for challenging the idea that leadership failure is primarily a problem of character, courage, or competence. His work instead examines how organizational design quietly shapes what decisions are possible, when judgment is allowed to surface, and where accountability ultimately lands. Much of his writing is concerned with the structural conditions under which people are asked to absorb consequences that systems refuse to hold.

Joel is the author of *Becoming Regenerative*, which was shortlisted by Thinkers50 for a Regenerative Business Award. That book explored regeneration as a leadership and organizational challenge rather than a branding exercise, and it marked the beginning of a longer inquiry into what regeneration actually costs when taken seriously.

Beyond his writing, Joel has served in advisory, executive, and board-level roles across a wide range of sectors, including energy, infrastructure, finance, and professional services. He is the founder of Green Project Management (GPM), where his work has focused on embedding sustainability and regenerative thinking into project, portfolio, and governance practices worldwide.

His frameworks and standards have been used by organizations seeking to move beyond performative sustainability toward structural change.

Joel writes from inside the systems he critiques. He has approved decisions that later proved impossible to stop, rewarded speed that narrowed judgment, and trusted processes that insulated harm. This book reflects not only his professional experience, but his ongoing reckoning with what it means to take responsibility once the design of a system is no longer invisible.

He lives in the United States and continues to write, advise, and speak on the limits of modern organizations and the conditions under which judgment can survive pressure.

How to Use This Book (Especially If You're Already Tired)

This is not a book about becoming a better hero.
It is a book about what your systems do to judgment long before you walk into the room.

If you read nothing else, read this: you cannot perform your way out of a design that quietly eats judgment and exports harm.

Who This Book Is For

Three kinds of people will recognize themselves here.

Board members and non-executive directors
You sit at the far end of the consequence chain and are told you still have control. You are held accountable for outcomes shaped long before decisions reach your

agenda, and you are asked to ratify what can no longer be unwound.

CEOs, C-suite, and executive teams
You inherit decisions that are "too far along to stop." You are praised for speed, punished for hesitation, and expected to absorb tensions the system refuses to hold.

Senior operators and system designers
You live inside the rooms where alignment, speed, and professionalism quietly replace judgment. You often know when something is wrong before anyone is willing to name it, and you are expected to make it work anyway.

If you do not recognize yourself in at least one of these, this book will probably irritate you more than help you. That, too, is information.

What This Book Is Actually About

This is a book about how systems decide before people do.

It traces how judgment is narrowed, displaced, and eventually designed out—through alignment, speed, silence, portfolios, assurance, authority without control, collapsing roles, and the disappearance of refusal. It then asks what would actually have to change for judgment to survive, and what that would cost.

This is not a manifesto for nicer leadership.
It is a pattern language for recognizing when your system has already decided—and a confrontation with what it would take to interrupt that inevitability.

How to Read It (Three Paths)

You can read this straight through.
If your time and attention are already overdrawn,
choose a path—and be honest about why.

Path 1: The Boardroom Path

If you are a board member, chair, or non-executive:

Start with:

- *What Do I Mean by Regenerative Leadership?*
- Chapter 1 – *The Ancient Error*
- Chapter 6 – *Authority Without Control*
- Chapter 8 – *When Portfolios Decide Before People Do*
- Chapter 9 – *Assurance as Safety*
- Chapter 11 – *The Real Cost of Regeneration*
- Chapter 13 – *The Responsibility of Knowing*

Read with one question in mind:
Where, in this chain, do we still genuinely have a choice—and where have we already accepted inevitability as professionalism?

Path 2: The Executive Team Path

If you are a CEO or part of an executive team:

Start with:

- *What Do I Mean by Regenerative Leadership?*
- Chapter 2 – *When Alignment Replaces Judgment*
- Chapter 3 – *Speed as a Design Constraint*
- Chapter 4 – *How Silence Is Learned*
- Chapter 5 – *Teams as Shock Absorbers*
- Chapter 10 – *Where Refusal Disappears*

- Chapter 12 – *What It Looks Like When Judgment Wins*

Read with one question in mind:
Which decisions in our world feel "already decided" before we enter the room—and who paid for that convenience?

Path 3: The Operator and System-Designer Path

If you run portfolios, functions, programs, or risk and assurance:

Start with:

- *What Do I Mean by Regenerative Leadership?*
- Chapter 3 – *Speed as a Design Constraint*
- Chapter 4 – *How Silence Is Learned*
- Chapter 5 – *Teams as Shock Absorbers*
- Chapter 8 – *When Portfolios Decide Before People Do*
- Chapter 9 – *Assurance as Safety*
- Chapter 11 – *The Real Cost of Regeneration*

Read with one question in mind:
Where, exactly, do we still have the right—and the structure—to stop? Not to raise a concern, but to refuse.

How to Work With This Book.

If you treat this as an interesting diagnosis, your system will absorb it and change nothing.

Instead, take one chapter into your next real meeting and ask:

"If this chapter is true, what on this agenda are we pretending is still a choice?"

Then choose **one** design move to test:

- a genuine stop rule with named conditions
- a protected dissent role
- a pre-committed board-level kill switch in one portfolio

Decide in advance what you are willing to give up. Do not talk about regeneration if speed, optionality, and deniability remain non-negotiable.

One Commitment Before You Start

Before you turn the page, choose:

- one room you already sit in (board, executive, portfolio, investment, risk), and
- one decision you know is coming in the next 6–12 months.

Read this book as if that decision is the test.

If nothing about how that decision is framed, paced, challenged, or stopped changes as a result, then this is just another leadership book you survived.

Is that what you want?

Table of Contents

What Do I Mean by Regenerative Leadership?

Regenerative is one of those words that has been stretched thin by overuse. It appears in strategy decks, conference themes, and vision statements, often standing in for a general sense of "better" without much clarity about what is actually different in practice. Before going any further, it is worth being precise about what this book means by the term.

Regenerative leadership is not about being nicer, greener, or more values-driven. It is not an advanced form of sustainability, and it is not a personal mindset. Regenerative leadership is about whether the systems you lead can restore their own capacity rather than consuming it. A regenerative system does not rely on exceptional people to compensate for structural weakness. It does not quietly burn through trust, energy, or judgment in order to meet short-term demands. It leaves the system with more ability to respond, adapt, and decide well than it had before.

By contrast, many leadership systems today are extractive, even when they are well intentioned. They extract attention, emotional labor, moral courage, and decision-making capacity from individuals, particularly leaders, to keep the system moving. They reward speed and alignment while externalizing the cost of that speed onto people who are expected to absorb it. Over time, these systems appear productive on the surface while steadily degrading the very capacities they depend on.

When leaders burn out, when teams become brittle, when decisions grow narrower and more defensive, those are not personal failures. They are symptoms of extractive design.

Regenerative leadership asks a different question. Not "How do we perform better?" but "What does this system do to the people inside it over time?" Not "Did we achieve the outcome?" but "What did it cost us to get there, and who paid that cost?" A system that repeatedly achieves its goals by concentrating strain in a few roles, or by suppressing disagreement until it reappears as crisis, is not regenerative, no matter how impressive its results look in the short term.

This distinction matters because regeneration is not something a leader can will into existence. It is not a matter of personal resilience, emotional intelligence, or ethical intent. It is a property of the system itself. Specifically, it is a property of how work is distributed, how decisions are constrained, and how teams are composed to handle pressure.

Most leadership failures are blamed on individuals who never had the authority to prevent them. I have been one of those individuals, held responsible for outcomes I could not meaningfully interrupt.

If this pattern feels familiar, it is worth asking a harder question. Not whether you have witnessed it, but whether you have benefited from it. Most people who operate inside these systems do. The system rewards those who adapt to it. It promotes them. It trusts them. Over time, it becomes difficult to distinguish professional success from participation in decisions whose consequences you no longer feel directly.

This is an observation drawn from watching the same pattern repeat across organizations, sectors, and cultures. When outcomes disappoint, we look for a leader. We ask who was in charge, who approved the decision, who failed to intervene. We replace people, restructure reporting lines, announce renewed commitments, and expect the system to behave differently. It rarely does.

What changes is the person at the front of the room. What stays largely intact is the structure behind them.

Leadership literature still treats the individual as the primary unit of success or failure. Leaders are trained, assessed, and corrected as if outcomes flow directly from personal competence or character. Teams are treated as neutral containers, something a leader "has" rather than something that actively shapes what is possible. That assumption might have held in simpler environments. It does not hold in complex systems where decisions emerge collectively and pressure is continuous.

Most senior leaders operate inside environments that are too fast-moving, too interconnected, and too constrained to be governed by individual capability alone. Silence, momentum, agreement, and hesitation are group behaviors before they are personal ones. Yet responsibility continues to concentrate upward, creating a structural mismatch between authority and accountability.

Over time, that mismatch extracts capacity. Leaders absorb what the system cannot hold. Teams adapt by avoiding friction. Decisions become smoother and weaker at the same time. Eventually, something gives.

This book is about that failure point. Not the moral failure of leaders, but the structural failure of teams that were never designed to be regenerative. It examines how team composition, role protection, and behavioral dynamics determine whether leadership depletes the system or leaves it stronger.

Leadership does not fail loudly. It fails quietly through teams that were never designed to carry what they were asked to hold.

Chapter 1

The Ancient Error

Every civilization tells itself the same story when things begin to fail. The details change, the language modernizes, the institutions grow more complex, but the story remains stubbornly intact. When decline becomes visible, when trust erodes, when systems no longer produce the outcomes they once did, societies search for individuals to blame. Kings are said to have grown weak. Generals are accused of arrogance or cowardice. Ministers are charged with corruption or incompetence. The remedy follows naturally. Remove the person. Replace the leader. Restore order.

This pattern is not accidental. It is one of the oldest political technologies humanity has developed. Personal blame provides emotional clarity in moments of collective uncertainty. It allows diffuse anxiety to be concentrated into a single figure. It transforms systemic strain into moral failure. Most importantly, it preserves the legitimacy of the underlying system by implying that the structure itself remains sound, requiring only better stewardship.

History records this maneuver with relentless consistency. The Roman Republic did not attribute its collapse to the design of its governing institutions. It blamed moral decay among its leaders, the ambition of individuals who no longer honored tradition. The French monarchy did not interpret revolution as the inevitable outcome of a brittle system unable to absorb economic and social pressure. It attributed unrest to bad advisors, to the indecision of the king, to the excesses of a court that had lost its way. Industrial catastrophes in the nineteenth century were explained as the result of careless workers or negligent managers, not as the predictable consequence of production systems designed to extract maximum output while externalizing risk.

I believed this explanation myself for years, including times when I approved leadership changes that felt decisive and responsible, and still watched the same failures repeat.

What is striking is not that these explanations were wrong, but that they were incomplete in precisely the same way. They focused on people because people are visible, narratable, and replaceable. Systems are none of those things. Systems are abstract, slow to change, and politically inconvenient to interrogate. Blaming leaders feels decisive. Redesigning institutions feels destabilizing.

This habit has survived every technological revolution. As organizations grew larger, faster, and more specialized, the tendency to personalize failure intensified rather than diminished. The complexity of modern systems made it increasingly difficult to trace causality in real time. When outcomes diverged from intention, leaders became the most legible point of intervention. Remove the executive. Replace the board. Announce reform. Move forward.

The persistence of this pattern should give us pause. If leadership quality were the primary determinant of institutional success, history would show clearer correlation between the replacement of leaders and the correction of outcomes. Instead, history shows cycles. New leaders arrive with intelligence, credibility, and resolve. For a time, confidence returns. Then the same pressures reassert themselves, the same compromises emerge, and the same failures reappear, often in forms eerily similar to those that preceded them.

This is not a failure of learning. It is a failure of framing.

Human beings are exquisitely sensitive to personal responsibility. We are far less equipped to perceive how structures shape behavior over time. The mind prefers agents to architectures, decisions to conditions, moments to trajectories. This cognitive bias is not a flaw. It is an evolutionary inheritance that allowed small groups to coordinate action long before abstract systems existed. In modern organizations, it becomes a liability.

As institutions scale, they create distance between decision and consequence. They fragment responsibility across roles, departments, and functions. They distribute knowledge unevenly and compress timeframes for action. Under these conditions, individual intent becomes a poor predictor of collective outcome. Systems begin to behave in ways that no single person intends, yet everyone participates in.

The ancient error lies in refusing to accept this reality.

When societies insist on treating systemic failure as personal failure, they obscure the mechanisms that actually govern behavior under pressure. They train themselves to look for stronger leaders rather than sturdier systems. They mistake decisiveness for control and confidence for capacity. Over time, this misdiagnosis hardens into ideology.

Modern leadership doctrine inherits this ideology wholesale. It celebrates heroic intervention, decisive action, and personal accountability while largely ignoring how organizational environments constrain what leaders can see, say, and do. Leaders are elevated rhetorically even as the systems around them narrow the range of acceptable judgment. When outcomes fail, leaders are punished for constraints they did not design, and the system is absolved by implication.

This is not accidental. It is functional.

Personal blame stabilizes institutions in the short term. It restores legitimacy without requiring structural change. It allows organizations to signal responsiveness while avoiding the deeper work of redesign. In doing so, it ensures that the same conditions will generate the same behaviors when pressure rises again.

History shows that civilizations collapse not when leaders fail to act, but when systems lose the capacity to adapt without scapegoating. The inability to distinguish between personal failure and structural failure is itself a form of decay. It marks the point at which institutions begin consuming their own leaders as a way to avoid confronting their limitations.

This book begins with that recognition because without it, everything that follows will be misread. If leadership failure remains the primary lens through which organizational breakdown is interpreted, then every solution will default to training, coaching, replacement, or exhortation. None of those interventions address the deeper question of how systems shape judgment before leaders ever have the chance to exercise it.

The chapters that follow will move forward in time, from ancient institutions to modern organizations, from empires to enterprises. But the core problem does not change. When pressure rises, systems simplify. When systems simplify, they narrow what can be seen and said. When that narrowing goes unexamined, failure becomes inevitable and personal blame becomes the only language available to explain it.

Before we can talk about regenerative teams, we have to confront the oldest habit in leadership thinking. The belief that replacing people fixes systems. History has already rendered its verdict on that belief. We continue to repeat it not because it works, but because it allows us to move on without changing what made failure likely in the first place.

The Modern Inheritance

The modern organization did not eliminate the ancient error. It perfected it.

As institutions industrialized and then digitized, they grew larger, faster, and more intricate than anything earlier societies had attempted to govern. Work became specialized. Decision making fragmented across functions, layers, and time zones. Information multiplied at a rate no individual could fully absorb. Authority was formalized. Responsibility was distributed. Accountability was documented. In theory, this architecture was meant to increase control. In practice, it introduced a new and more dangerous illusion.

Modern organizations confuse coordination with comprehension.

The belief that systems can be managed through decomposition is foundational to contemporary management. Break the work into parts. Assign clear roles. Define interfaces. Establish reporting lines. Measure performance. Review outcomes. This logic has delivered extraordinary productivity and scale. It has also created environments in which no one fully sees the whole, and where decisions are made at the edge of partial information under escalating pressure.

In such environments, failure rarely arrives as a dramatic rupture. It arrives as drift.

Small tradeoffs accumulate. Margins erode. Exceptions become routines. What once felt provisional becomes permanent. Each adjustment makes sense locally, even responsibly, within the frame of the role making it. The danger lies not in any single decision, but in the system's growing inability to integrate the consequences of those decisions across time and space.

The modern organization does not collapse because people stop caring. It collapses because caring is no longer sufficient to overcome the way work is structured.

As scale increased, so did distance. Decision makers moved further from the physical, human, and ecological consequences of their choices. Feedback loops lengthened. Signals weakened. Harm became abstracted into reports, metrics, and lagging indicators. By the time impact was visible, it was often already entrenched.

To compensate, organizations layered on process.

Governance frameworks proliferated. Risk registers expanded. Assurance functions multiplied. Compliance regimes hardened. These mechanisms were not cynical. They were rational responses to complexity. Yet they introduced a subtle shift in how responsibility was experienced. Judgment began to migrate from lived awareness to documented procedure. The question became not whether a decision was wise, but whether it complied with the established process.

Process became a proxy for safety. Documentation became a substitute for understanding.

This is where the ancient error adapted to modern form. When outcomes failed, organizations could now point not only to individuals, but to completed checklists, approved models, and documented reviews. The system appeared diligent even as it lost the ability to notice what mattered most.

Speed accelerated this dynamic.

Modern markets reward rapid execution. Competitive advantage is often framed in terms of time. First to market. Faster than rivals. Agile. Lean. Responsive. These concepts are not inherently destructive. But under sustained competitive pressure, speed begins to function as an environmental constant rather than a variable. Once speed becomes non-negotiable, everything else must adapt to it.

Including judgment.

In fast systems, complexity is a liability. Ambiguity slows decisions. Dissent introduces friction. Nuance resists compression. Over time, organizations learn to treat these qualities not as signals to pause, but as obstacles to overcome. They invest heavily in tools and language designed to simplify reality without stopping motion.

Risk is not ignored. It is reframed.

Uncertainty is not denied. It is bounded.

Disagreement is not prohibited. It is redirected.

The modern organization becomes extraordinarily skilled at converting messy reality into forms that can move through its decision machinery. This skill is celebrated as professionalism. It is rewarded. It is taught. It becomes cultural.

What is lost in the process is not information, but texture.

Under these conditions, leaders inherit a paradoxical role. They are held accountable for outcomes that emerge from systems designed to move faster than reflective judgment allows. They are expected to intervene decisively, even as the structure of work constrains what reaches them and when. They are praised for confidence and penalized for hesitation, even when hesitation would be the more responsible response.

The leader becomes both symbol and sink.

This dynamic explains why leadership roles feel increasingly heavy even as formal authority grows. Leaders are asked to absorb unresolved tension that the system cannot carry. They become the focal point for anxiety, expectation, and consequence. When outcomes fail, the pressure to locate blame finds its most convenient target.

The system survives.
The leader does not.

Modern management theory often frames this as a gap in capability. Leaders need better information. Better dashboards. Better training. Better values. These prescriptions assume that the primary constraint lies at the level of the individual. They leave largely unexamined the way organizational design itself shapes what is possible under pressure.

History suggests a different reading. As organizations grew more complex, they did not outgrow the ancient error. They embedded it more deeply into structure, language, and process. Personal blame remained the preferred explanatory tool because it scaled better than systemic accountability.

The result is a peculiar form of institutional blindness. Organizations become adept at diagnosing failure after the fact, while remaining poor at recognizing the conditions that make failure likely in advance. They reward compliance with process rather than confrontation of reality. They valorize leaders who can carry pressure quietly, even when that pressure signals a deeper design flaw.

This is why modern collapses feel so baffling and yet so familiar. The warning signs are present. The intelligence exists. The people involved are capable and often deeply committed. And still the system moves forward along a narrowing path until the cost becomes undeniable.

At that point, the ancient ritual resumes. A leader is replaced. Confidence returns. The cycle resets.

What has changed from earlier eras is not the pattern, but the speed and scale at which it now operates. Modern organizations can move from early signal to catastrophic outcome in compressed timeframes. Digital systems amplify both efficiency and error. Global reach multiplies impact. The stakes are no longer local or contained.

This is why the ancient error has become more dangerous, not less.

Before we can examine how teams function inside this environment, we have to sit with the uncomfortable inheritance modern organizations carry. They are built to optimize movement, not meaning. They excel at execution, not reflection. Under pressure, they simplify reality in ways that feel rational and responsible until the consequences accumulate beyond denial.

Before collapse, there is almost always a quieter moment.

The Moment the Language Changes

The document had been revised three times already.

It began life as a stop. Not an alarm, not a crisis declaration, just a clear statement that proceeding as planned introduced a level of risk that could not be responsibly absorbed under the current conditions. The person who wrote it had spent years learning how to phrase such concerns in ways that would be taken seriously. The language was careful. The analysis was conservative. The conclusion was narrow. Delay was recommended, not cancellation, and only long enough to address a specific set of unresolved issues.

By the time the document reached the review meeting, its tone had softened.

The core facts were still present, but the framing had shifted. What was once described as a condition that required resolution was now presented as a scenario that could be mitigated. The word stop no longer appeared. It had been replaced with monitor. The recommendation to delay had become a suggestion to proceed with enhanced oversight.

No one had asked for this change directly. It had emerged through conversation, through questions about schedule impact, through reminders about commitments already made, through casual remarks about the difficulty of explaining another delay to people who were not in the room. Each edit felt reasonable on its own. Each one made the document easier to move forward.

The author noticed the change immediately. They also noticed the room.

The meeting was full. Senior people were present. Time was limited. The agenda was already behind. When the document was discussed, the revised language fit smoothly into the conversation. Questions were asked. Assurances were offered. Mitigations were noted. The unresolved issues were acknowledged without being allowed to dominate.

At one point, the author considered intervening. They knew exactly which sentence had shifted the meaning. They knew that the risk, as now described, no longer reflected their original assessment. They also knew what would follow if they insisted on restoring the earlier language. The discussion would stall. The room would turn toward justification rather than decision. Attention would move from the issue itself to the person raising it.

They had seen this before.

So they said nothing.

The decision was approved. The meeting moved on. Afterward, several people thanked the author for being pragmatic, for helping the team find a way forward without unnecessary disruption. Someone remarked that this was exactly the kind of judgment the organization needed more of.

Weeks later, when the issue surfaced in a more visible form, the original document was retrieved. It was cited as evidence that the risk had been identified and managed. The revised language was now part of the record. The author read it again and recognized their own words, altered just enough to belong to the system rather than to their original intent.

When the review concluded, the findings noted that the concern had been raised, documented, and addressed according to process. No one suggested that the process itself had transformed the concern into something it was never meant to be. The author was not blamed. They were not even mentioned.

They carried the outcome quietly, along with the knowledge that the moment when a different choice was possible had passed not through malice or neglect, but through professionalism.

The Room Where It Happens

The most consequential decisions in organizations are almost never made in moments of crisis. They are made in rooms that feel controlled, professional, and familiar, by people who believe they are doing their jobs well. These rooms rarely appear in postmortems or histories because nothing dramatic happens inside them. There is no raised voice, no ethical standoff, no moment that feels decisive in retrospect. What happens instead is quieter and far more powerful. Reality is shaped into a form the organization can tolerate, and once that shaping is complete, the decision becomes almost automatic.

The room is not remarkable. It may be a conference room, a virtual meeting, a review session, or a steering committee. The agenda has been circulated in advance. Materials are prepared according to established templates. Data has been summarized, assumptions clarified, risks listed, dependencies identified. Everyone present understands the purpose of the meeting and the constraints under which it operates. Time is limited. Momentum matters. There is an implicit expectation that progress will be made.

No one arrives intending to be reckless. No one arrives planning to ignore risk or dismiss consequences. Most of the people in the room are competent, conscientious, and experienced. Many have spent years navigating similar decisions without incident. That history matters, because it shapes what feels reasonable now.

As the discussion begins, information flows in an orderly way. Updates are delivered. Metrics are reviewed. Questions are asked and answered within the bounds of what the data can support. When uncertainty appears, it is acknowledged and contained. Language becomes important here, not because anyone is manipulating it deliberately, but because language is the primary tool the organization has for converting complexity into action.

Risks are discussed, but in categories that make them manageable. Probabilities are assigned. Impacts are estimated. Mitigations are noted. Each step reduces ambiguity and moves the conversation closer to closure. This process is not dishonest. It is procedural. It reflects the organization's need to act despite incomplete information.

At some point, however, a tension emerges that does not fit neatly into the available categories. It may be a concern about interaction effects, about second order consequences, about how multiple small risks might compound under certain conditions. It may be an unease that cannot yet be articulated clearly, because it sits between disciplines or outside the current scope of analysis. It is not a fully formed objection, but it is also not nothing.

Someone notices.

Often, more than one person notices. But noticing is not the same as speaking, and speaking is not the same as being heard. To raise the concern in a way that matters, it must be translated into the language the room can accept. It must fit within the time available. It must be framed as actionable rather than destabilizing. It must not derail the decision unless the organization is prepared to pay the cost of delay.

This is where the narrowing accelerates.

The concern is raised tentatively, often as a question rather than a statement. It is acknowledged politely. It is discussed briefly. Then it is either folded into an existing risk category or deferred for later consideration. The system has learned how to do this smoothly. It does not reject the concern. It absorbs it.

From the outside, this looks like responsible governance. Risks were identified. Questions were asked. Responses were recorded. From the inside, something more subtle has happened. The concern has been reshaped into a form that allows the decision to proceed without interruption.

No one says that the question is unwelcome. No one needs to. The organization has already taught its people, over many prior decisions, how much friction is acceptable and when it becomes a problem. That learning is not written down. It is embodied. People carry it with them into the room.

As the discussion continues, the options on the table begin to converge. The range of possible actions narrows. What remains are variations that differ in degree, not in kind. The decision starts to feel inevitable, not because it is the only possible choice, but because alternatives now appear increasingly impractical within the constraints that have been accepted as given.

This is the moment where many people later say they would have spoken up. It is also the moment when speaking up feels least effective.

The concern, if raised forcefully now, would require revisiting assumptions that have already been tacitly accepted. It would introduce delay into a process that is expected to move forward. It would require explaining to people outside the room why progress has stalled. It would shift attention from execution to uncertainty, from action to doubt.

In organizations that prize speed, that shift carries risk of its own.

The individual considering whether to press the issue is not calculating moral tradeoffs in the abstract. They are navigating a web of professional consequences that have been reinforced over time. They know what happens to people who consistently slow things down without offering clear alternatives. They know how questions can be reinterpreted as lack of alignment, lack of confidence, or lack of readiness for senior responsibility. They may also know that the concern they feel cannot yet be supported by data strong enough to withstand scrutiny.

The system does not need to silence them. It has already taught them how to silence themselves.

When the decision is finally reached, it feels like a conclusion rather than a choice. The remaining uncertainties are noted and accepted. Mitigations are assigned. Next steps are agreed upon. The meeting ends on time. People leave with the sense that something important has been accomplished.

And in a narrow sense, it has.

The organization has maintained momentum. It has acted decisively. It has preserved coherence under pressure. These are not trivial achievements. They are the very qualities modern institutions are built to produce.

What has been lost is harder to name. It is not a fact or a data point. It is the capacity of the system to remain open to discomfort long enough for a different decision to emerge.

That capacity erodes gradually. Each time the organization resolves tension by narrowing rather than exploring, it reinforces the behavior. Each time it rewards progress over pause, it teaches its people what matters most. Over time, the room becomes very good at producing decisions that feel reasonable, defensible, and aligned with institutional expectations, even when they carry risks no one fully owns.

This is why later reviews so often conclude that the information was available. It was. What was unavailable was the space to hold that information without forcing it into premature closure.

When failure finally becomes visible, the room is long gone. The people involved remember fragments. They recall unease, time pressure, incomplete analysis. They struggle to explain why they did not insist, because in retrospect the insistence seems obvious. What they rarely articulate is how the decision process itself made insistence feel impractical at the time.

From the outside, it looks like a failure of courage. From the inside, it felt like professionalism.

This is the most dangerous illusion modern organizations produce. The belief that responsible behavior within a flawed decision environment will somehow yield responsible outcomes. It allows systems to continue operating without questioning the conditions under which judgment is exercised.

By the time the consequences surface, the system has already moved on. The decision has been implemented. The effects are unfolding. Attention shifts to response rather than prevention. Accountability searches for a name.

The room where the decision was shaped never appears in the final report. It cannot, because nothing illegal or overtly wrong occurred there. The narrowing was gradual, collective, and rational within the context of the system. There is no single moment to point to, no dramatic exchange to quote.

And yet, that room is where the outcome was decided.

Not because anyone chose failure, but because the system could no longer tolerate the conditions required to choose differently.

Why Replacement Feels Like Resolution

When failure finally becomes undeniable, attention shifts away from the room where the decision was shaped and toward the figure most easily associated with its outcome. This shift feels natural, even necessary. Organizations need closure. Stakeholders demand accountability. Regulators, boards, investors, employees, and the public all look for a clear answer to a simple question: who was responsible.

Modern organizations are well practiced at providing one.

Leadership accountability offers a clean narrative. It personalizes complexity. It converts diffuse systemic strain into an individual story that can be told, explained, and concluded. The leader is named, assessed, and removed. The organization signals seriousness. Confidence begins to return. People believe that the problem has been addressed because something visible has changed.

What rarely follows is an examination of why that leader was placed in a position where failure was increasingly likely regardless of intent or competence.

Replacement works at the level of emotion. It restores order without requiring the organization to confront its own design. It allows the system to preserve its identity while sacrificing one of its visible representatives. This trade is not accidental. It is efficient. It stabilizes institutions in moments of crisis and allows work to continue.

It also ensures recurrence.

When a leader is removed, the organization often describes the event as learning. Processes are reviewed. Training is refreshed. Values are reaffirmed. Sometimes new controls are added. Yet the deeper conditions that shaped the original decision remain largely intact. Speed continues to dominate. Incentives remain aligned to momentum. Decision structures continue to reward closure over exploration. The capacity to hold unresolved tension is not strengthened. It is deferred.

The next leader inherits the same corridors of acceptability, the same pressure gradients, and the same unspoken expectations. They arrive determined to do better, and often they do, for a time. Early wins reinforce confidence. The system appears responsive. Then the familiar pressures return, and with them the same narrowing of reality.

History is littered with examples of this cycle, but organizations rarely interpret it as structural failure. They interpret it as unfortunate repetition. Another leader who did not quite rise to the moment. Another missed opportunity. Another lesson learned too late.

This interpretation is comforting because it preserves a fundamental belief. That leadership operates above the system rather than within it. That the right person, properly trained and sufficiently courageous, can overcome constraints that are largely invisible until they are violated.

That belief is false.

Leaders do not operate outside systems. They are produced by them, selected by them, rewarded by them, and constrained by them. They may have influence, but that influence is exercised within boundaries the system defines. When pressure rises, those boundaries harden. What was once flexible becomes fixed. What was once discussable becomes disruptive. What was once possible becomes impractical.

In such environments, leadership is not a position of control. It is a position of concentration. Authority concentrates there. Expectation concentrates there. Consequence concentrates there. What does not concentrate there is full visibility into how decisions are shaped before they reach the leader's desk.

This is why leadership roles feel increasingly punishing even as they are increasingly celebrated. Leaders are expected to absorb ambiguity the organization cannot hold, to resolve tensions the system refuses to confront, and to take responsibility for outcomes shaped by many hands under conditions they did not design. Burnout, isolation, and failure at the top are not signs of individual weakness. They are indicators of systemic overload.

Replacing leaders does not reduce that load. It redistributes it.

Modern leadership discourse often responds to this reality by calling for greater resilience. Leaders must be tougher, more adaptive, more emotionally intelligent. They must listen better, communicate more clearly, and remain calm under pressure. These qualities are valuable, but they do not address the central issue. They assume the problem is the leader's capacity to endure rather than the system's capacity to function.

Endurance is not a strategy. It is a stopgap.

What organizations consistently fail to examine is the relationship between speed, structure, and judgment. They do not ask how much uncertainty their decision processes can actually tolerate. They do not assess whether their teams are designed to surface disagreement without penalty or whether dissent is merely permitted in theory and punished in practice. They do not evaluate whether governance constrains decisions before harm occurs or simply documents them afterward.

These questions are uncomfortable because they do not point to simple remedies. They implicate design choices that sit deep within organizational identity. They challenge assumptions about efficiency, competitiveness, and control. They require slowing down in environments that equate speed with competence and hesitation with weakness.

It is far easier to replace a leader.

This is why replacement continues to feel like resolution even as it fails to produce change. It offers narrative closure without demanding structural courage. It allows organizations to move forward without altering the conditions that make forward motion dangerous.

The cost of this avoidance accumulates over time. Each cycle of replacement reinforces the belief that the problem lies in people rather than in design. Each failure teaches the system that it can survive by consuming its leaders. Each success, narrowly defined, reinforces the patterns that make failure more likely later.

By the time organizations begin to question this logic, the damage is often already done.

This book does not begin with answers because answers offered too early would simply repeat the same error in a different form. It begins by removing a belief that has outlived its usefulness. The belief that leadership change alone can correct systemic failure. The belief that better people will compensate for brittle design. The belief that responsibility can be concentrated without distorting judgment.

What remains, once that belief is stripped away, is an uncomfortable recognition. That the real work of leadership does not begin with individuals at the top, but with the conditions under which teams make decisions long before leaders are asked to approve them.

Until those conditions are understood, every attempt to build regenerative teams will collapse into familiar patterns. Alignment will continue to substitute for agreement. Speed will continue to override judgment. Accountability will continue to concentrate where control is weakest.

History has already shown us where this leads. Modern organizations are not exempt from that lesson. They are simply faster, more complex, and capable of causing greater harm in shorter timeframes.

If this chapter has done its work, it has removed the reader's last safe distance from the problem. There is no longer a clear villain to blame or a simple solution to adopt. What remains is the recognition that failure is often decided quietly, collectively, and long before it becomes visible.

The chapters that follow do not ask how to become a better leader. They ask how to build teams and organizations that can hold disagreement, uncertainty, and consequence without collapsing into premature certainty or personal blame.

That work begins not with replacement, but with redesign.

The Cost We Keep Deferring

When systems decide before people do, the cost is never theoretical. It is simply displaced.

The language of modern organizations allows harm to travel without being named. Decisions are described as tradeoffs, risks are categorized as acceptable, and impacts are projected forward into reports and scenarios that soften their immediacy. In this language, no one chooses damage. It arrives later, downstream, diluted by distance and time. By the time it becomes visible, it belongs to someone else.

This is how harm moves through institutions without triggering refusal.

Workers absorb it first. They carry safety risk framed as operational necessity. They carry moral injury when they are asked to implement decisions they privately question but cannot realistically challenge. They carry exhaustion as systems demand resilience rather than redesign. When something goes wrong, they are described as insufficiently trained, insufficiently vigilant, or insufficiently aligned. Their proximity to consequence makes them convenient recipients of blame.

Communities absorb it next. Environmental degradation is framed as externality. Infrastructure decisions lock in vulnerability that will surface decades later. Housing, water, health, and mobility systems inherit fragility that no single project appears responsible for creating. When the impact arrives, it is treated as unfortunate, unintended, and too complex to assign clean accountability.

Ecosystems absorb it silently. Damage accumulates slowly enough to remain compatible with quarterly reporting, yet rapidly enough to exceed recovery thresholds before institutions acknowledge what has been lost. Once those limits are crossed, remediation is rebranded as innovation, and irreversible loss is treated as the cost of progress.

Trust absorbs what remains. Trust in institutions. Trust in leadership. Trust in the promise that systems are designed to protect people rather than consume them. Once trust collapses, it does not regenerate on command. It leaves behind compliance without commitment, participation without belief, and governance without legitimacy.

These are not failures of intent. They are failures of structure.

Systems that decide before people do are efficient at moving work forward. They are also efficient at pushing consequence into places that lack the power to refuse it. Over time, this creates a moral asymmetry that organizations rarely acknowledge. Decisions are made at a distance. Consequences are felt up close. Accountability concentrates upward only after damage becomes undeniable, and even then it rarely reaches the conditions that made the decision inevitable.

Leadership replacement does nothing to interrupt this flow. It signals seriousness while preserving the pathways through which harm travels. It allows organizations to demonstrate accountability without assuming responsibility for design. It reassures stakeholders that someone has paid a price, even as the system prepares to produce the next failure.

This is why repetition is not accidental. It is engineered.

The cost of deferral compounds. Each cycle of decision compression makes the next cycle easier. Each instance of displaced harm normalizes the practice. Each leader removed without structural change reinforces the lesson that endurance is expected and refusal is impractical. Over time, organizations become dependent on this dynamic. They function by extracting resilience from people and places that cannot opt out.

At a certain point, the system no longer needs explicit permission to do this. It has learned.

This is the moment most leadership literature avoids. The moment when it becomes clear that the problem is not insufficient courage, insufficient values, or insufficient skill. The problem is that the organization has become structurally incapable of choosing differently without first confronting its own design.

That confrontation is costly. It requires slowing systems that equate speed with competence. It requires surfacing disagreement that has been carefully trained out of meetings. It requires acknowledging that some decisions should not proceed, even when they are technically feasible and economically attractive. It requires accepting that leadership is not a role to be strengthened indefinitely, but a function that must be supported by teams capable of carrying tension rather than displacing it.

Most organizations are not prepared for this work. They continue to invest in people while leaving structures untouched. They continue to train leaders to endure rather than redesign. They continue to celebrate resilience while treating fragility as a personal flaw instead of a systemic signal.

History shows where this path leads. Institutions that cannot interrupt their own momentum eventually mistake motion for progress and stability for health. When collapse comes, it is described as sudden. It is never sudden for those who have been carrying the cost all along.

This book does not begin with optimism. It begins with responsibility.

Not responsibility as blame, but responsibility as the willingness to see where consequence actually lands and to stop pretending that replacement is the same as change. Until organizations confront the cost of systems that decide before people do, every attempt to build regenerative teams will be constrained by the same invisible limits.

The chapters that follow do not ask how to make leaders stronger. They ask how to design teams and organizations that can hold disagreement, uncertainty, and consequence without exporting harm to those least able to refuse it.

If that question feels uncomfortable, it should. Comfort has been subsidized for a long time. The bill is now coming due.

Chapter 2

When Alignment Replaces Judgment

Alignment is treated as a moral achievement.

Organizations praise it, reward it, and measure it as evidence of health. Leaders are taught to build it. Teams are assessed by it. Disagreement is tolerated only insofar as it can be resolved into a shared position within acceptable timeframes. Once alignment is reached, decisions move forward with confidence, and any remaining doubt is reframed as risk already considered.

This framing feels responsible. It signals cohesion. It reassures stakeholders that the organization knows what it is doing.

It is also one of the most reliable ways systems teach themselves not to think.

Alignment is not the same as judgment. It is an outcome, not a capability. Judgment is the capacity to hold competing interpretations of reality long enough for consequences to become visible. Alignment collapses that holding space. It resolves difference into movement. Once achieved, it becomes self-justifying. If everyone agrees, the decision must be sound.

This is how alignment quietly replaces discernment.

In well-functioning teams, disagreement is not a problem to be solved. It is a signal to be explored. It indicates that reality is more complex than any single framing can capture. It slows the rush to closure and forces attention onto assumptions that would otherwise remain unexamined.

Alignment interrupts that process. It rewards convergence over accuracy. It privileges coherence over correctness. It treats shared belief as evidence of truth.

Under pressure, this substitution accelerates.

Most organizations operate in environments where delay carries visible cost. Opportunities are framed as fleeting. Risks are framed as manageable. Time becomes a constraint that shapes not just what decisions are made, but how much complexity they are allowed to contain. In these conditions, alignment becomes more than desirable. It becomes necessary.

Disagreement slows things down.
Questions introduce friction.
Uncertainty complicates accountability.

Alignment restores motion.

The shift is subtle. No one announces it. No policy changes are required. Teams learn through experience which behaviors are rewarded and which ones are quietly penalized. Questions that open new lines of inquiry are welcomed early, then discouraged as timelines tighten. Concerns that complicate delivery are reframed as issues already addressed. Dissent that cannot be resolved is deferred, softened, or absorbed into language that allows the decision to proceed.

Over time, alignment becomes a proxy for professionalism.

People learn how to express doubt in ways that do not disrupt momentum. They learn how to ask questions that signal engagement without reopening decisions. They learn which concerns are worth raising and which ones will be interpreted as lack of readiness or poor judgment. This learning is not explicit. It is situational. It is reinforced through tone, timing, and response.

The result is not silence. It is agreement.

Agreement that feels earned. Agreement that feels responsible. Agreement that carries the appearance of collective intelligence.

What it lacks is resistance.

Judgment requires friction. It requires the ability to tolerate unresolved tension without forcing resolution. It requires structures that protect minority views long enough for their implications to be tested. Alignment short circuits that process. It compresses complexity into a form that can move forward.

This compression is rarely malicious. It is efficient.

Teams under pressure do not abandon judgment because they no longer care. They abandon it because the system no longer has space to hold it. Alignment offers relief. It reduces uncertainty. It distributes responsibility. Once everyone agrees, no one stands alone.

This is why alignment feels safe.

It is also why it is dangerous.

The Meeting That Ended Early

The meeting was scheduled for ninety minutes. By the forty-minute mark, the decision was already made.

It did not feel rushed. In fact, several people remarked on how efficient the discussion had been. The agenda was clear. The materials were familiar. The options had been narrowed in advance. When the conversation began, everyone understood the direction of travel.

There had been disagreement earlier. It had surfaced in pre-reads, in side conversations, in questions sent ahead of time. Alternative approaches were circulated. Risks were noted. Assumptions were challenged. The team had done what it considered its due diligence.

By the time they were in the room together, the tone had shifted.

The first few comments were exploratory. Someone asked about second-order impacts. Someone else raised a dependency that had not been fully resolved. The responses were calm, confident, and reassuring. Those issues were acknowledged, then placed within the broader framing of progress already achieved.

We have considered that.
We can manage it.
It does not change the overall recommendation.

Heads nodded. No one objected.

As the discussion continued, the remaining questions became smaller. Clarifications rather than challenges. Details rather than direction. Each answer tightened the frame rather than reopening it. The sense of convergence grew.

At one point, someone hesitated.

They had been quiet for most of the meeting, listening carefully. They understood the case being made. They also understood what had not been said. There was an interaction effect between two of the identified risks that had not been explored. Individually, each was manageable. Together, they created a condition that felt different.

They considered raising it.

The meeting was moving well. Time was being saved. The group was aligned. Introducing a new line of inquiry now would require stepping backward. It would complicate a decision that felt nearly complete. It would require explaining why an issue not surfaced earlier was suddenly important.

They decided to wait.

The decision was finalized shortly after. The chair summarized the rationale clearly. The risks were acknowledged. The mitigations were assigned. Everyone agreed. The meeting ended early.

Several people commented on how well the team worked together. Someone mentioned that this was a good example of alignment done right. Another noted that it was refreshing to see a group reach consensus without getting stuck in unnecessary debate.

No one mentioned the hesitation.

Weeks later, when the interaction effect surfaced in practice, it was treated as an unfortunate complication. The documentation was reviewed. The original risks were present. The mitigations had been reasonable. There was no single moment where a mistake could be identified.

In hindsight, the decision still made sense.

What could not be recovered was the moment when judgment might have slowed alignment just enough to notice what the system had compressed.

Alignment does not fail loudly. It succeeds too quickly.

Aligned teams can move fast in the wrong direction without noticing. They can generate confidence without clarity. They can mistake consensus for correctness and momentum for progress. When outcomes fail, the presence of alignment becomes evidence that the decision was reasonable at the time.

Everyone agreed.

That sentence carries extraordinary power in post-hoc review. It dissolves accountability into collectivity. It reframes failure as unforeseeable rather than as the predictable outcome of prematurely resolved disagreement.

What disappears in that narrative is the moment when alternatives were still visible.

In most organizations, there is a brief window early in decision processes when divergence is tolerated. Ideas compete. Scenarios are explored. Risks are surfaced. This phase is often described as healthy debate. It is encouraged rhetorically. Then, without formal transition, the expectation shifts.

Now we need alignment.

The shift is rarely announced, but it is felt. Questions that were welcomed minutes earlier now slow progress. Concerns that once signaled diligence now threaten closure. The team moves from exploration to convergence, not because understanding has been achieved, but because the system requires a decision.

This is the moment judgment is most vulnerable.

The pressure to align does not eliminate disagreement. It redirects it. Concerns are translated into language that fits existing frames. Dissent becomes conditional. Objections are softened into suggestions. Risks are acknowledged without being allowed to dominate.

What remains is a shared position that feels collective but may not be considered.

Teams learn to live inside this pattern. They become adept at reaching alignment quickly. They celebrate it as maturity. They describe it as trust. They rarely ask what was lost in the process.

When alignment replaces judgment, failure does not arrive as surprise. It arrives as explanation.

The explanation is always coherent. The rationale is well documented. The decision path makes sense when read linearly. What cannot be reconstructed is the complexity that was present before alignment collapsed it.

This is why organizations with strong alignment cultures often struggle to learn from failure. The very mechanisms that produced alignment also produced the narrative that defends it. Decisions were made responsibly. Risks were considered. Agreement was achieved. The system did what it was designed to do.

What it was not designed to do was remain open long enough for judgment to mature.

This chapter is not an argument against alignment. Alignment is necessary for action. Teams cannot remain perpetually divergent. Decisions must be made.

The problem begins when alignment is treated as evidence of quality rather than as a phase to be navigated carefully.

Regenerative teams do not reject alignment. They delay it.

They understand that judgment requires time, friction, and protection from premature closure. They design decision processes that distinguish between convergence needed for action and divergence needed for understanding. They recognize that the cost of early alignment is not visible until much later, when options have already collapsed and consequences can no longer be avoided.

Most teams are not designed to make that distinction. They are designed to move.

The next chapter examines what happens when speed becomes the dominant design constraint, and why even well-intentioned teams lose the capacity to pause

once motion is rewarded more consistently than
accuracy.

Chapter 3

Speed as a Design Constraint

Speed is treated as competence.

Organizations reward it, promote it, and equate it with seriousness. Fast teams are described as decisive. Fast leaders are described as strong. Deliberation is tolerated early, but only as long as it does not threaten delivery. Once motion begins, slowing down requires justification. Continuing does not.

I've rewarded people for moving quickly under pressure and penalized those who slowed decisions down, long before I understood what that trade was actually doing to judgment.

This framing feels rational. Markets move quickly. Opportunities close. Competitors do not wait. Delay carries visible cost, while caution carries reputational risk. In this environment, speed appears neutral, even necessary.

It is not.

Speed is not simply how fast work moves. It is a design condition that shapes what kinds of decisions can be made at all. When speed becomes non-negotiable, it stops being a strategy and becomes an environment. Once that happens, judgment adapts around it.

This is where teams begin to lose the ability to pause.

Alignment collapses difference. Speed collapses time. One produces agreement that feels responsible. The other produces continuation that feels inevitable.

Most organizations do not experience this shift as a choice. No one declares that speed now matters more than accuracy, or that continuation matters more than consequence. The transition is gradual. It emerges through pressure, incentives, and repeated reinforcement. Over time, the organization teaches itself that stopping is dangerous.

Not because stopping is wrong, but because stopping interrupts motion the system depends on.

In early stages of work, uncertainty is tolerated. Exploration is encouraged. Alternatives are discussed. Teams are invited to think broadly, to surface risks, to consider long-term effects. This phase is often described as strategic.

Then something changes.

Commitments are made. Timelines are published. Resources are allocated. Dependencies form. At that point, uncertainty begins to carry a different meaning. It no longer signals diligence. It signals risk to momentum. Questions that once expanded understanding now threaten delay. Reflection becomes reinterpreted as hesitation.

The organization has not decided to stop thinking. It has decided to keep moving.

This is the moment speed becomes a constraint rather than a preference.

Under these conditions, teams do not resolve uncertainty. They compress it. Unknowns are translated into assumptions that allow work to proceed. Risks are reframed as manageable. Gaps in understanding are deferred. The system learns how to move forward without requiring clarity.

This adaptation is not reckless. It is professional.

People learn which questions are acceptable once motion is underway. They learn how to frame concerns so they do not disrupt progress. They learn that some issues can be raised early, but should not be reopened later. The longer work is in motion, the narrower the space for interruption becomes.

Speed creates momentum. Momentum creates dependency. Dependency creates irreversibility.

By the time teams realize they should slow down, stopping has already become expensive.

This is not about rushing. Many of the most damaging decisions are made carefully, with detailed analysis and extensive documentation. The problem is not haste. The problem is that motion itself becomes the default decision.

Once work is moving, continuation requires no argument. Stopping does.

This asymmetry matters.

In fast systems, continuation is framed as neutral. Pausing is framed as active intervention. To slow down is to introduce friction into a process designed to minimize it. The burden of proof shifts. Those who want to stop must explain why. Those who want to continue do not.

This inversion quietly reshapes responsibility.

Early in a decision process, the question is often "should we proceed?" Later, it becomes "how do we manage what we have already started?" The shift happens without announcement, but it is decisive. Once the frame changes, judgment narrows. The range of acceptable options collapses.

Teams begin to behave as if momentum itself were evidence of correctness.

This is why speed feels productive even when it degrades decision quality. Movement creates the appearance of progress. Deliverables accumulate. Milestones are reached. Activity becomes visible. Reflection, by contrast, leaves little trace. It produces no artifacts that signal value to the system.

In environments that measure performance through output, speed wins by default.

The cost of this bias is not immediately visible. In fact, speed often delivers short-term success. Projects launch. Products ship. Decisions are executed. The organization appears responsive and capable. It is only later, when consequences surface, that the cost becomes clear.

By then, it is too late to reverse course.

Speed does not eliminate choice. It delays it.

Decisions that should have been made explicitly are made implicitly through continuation. Options that should have been evaluated are removed through dependency. Risks that should have been confronted are absorbed through momentum. What remains is a narrowing path that feels inevitable.

This is how motion replaces choice.

The Point of No Pause

The work had been underway for months.

The initial decision had not been controversial. It made sense at the time. The opportunity was real. The market signal was strong. The organization had the capability. Early analysis supported the move. Leadership approved the plan with appropriate caution and clear conditions.

Those conditions mattered early. They framed the work. They shaped early milestones. Teams were encouraged to surface risks and report concerns as they emerged. Governance checkpoints were scheduled. The language of review was present.

Then the work began.

Progress was steady. Timelines were met. Dependencies were established. External partners were engaged. Internal teams aligned their plans around the new initiative. Budgets were committed. Reputations became attached.

At one of the scheduled reviews, a concern surfaced.

It was not new information. It was an interaction between two known factors that had not previously been considered together. Individually, each was manageable. Together, they introduced a vulnerability that would be difficult to address once the next phase began.

The team presenting the update acknowledged the issue. They explained that it was being monitored. Mitigations were identified. None of them were unreasonable.

Someone asked whether this was a moment to pause.

The question landed awkwardly. Not because it was inappropriate, but because it introduced the only kind of risk the room could not manage, the risk of looking unprepared to proceed. Pausing would mean revisiting assumptions that were already embedded in schedules, contracts, and commitments. It would require explaining delay to stakeholders who had been promised progress. It would raise questions about decisions already endorsed.

The discussion shifted quickly.

The concern was reframed as something that could be managed downstream. The cost of stopping was noted implicitly. The cost of continuing was harder to articulate. The group agreed to proceed, with enhanced monitoring and a promise to revisit if conditions changed.

No one objected.

After the meeting, several participants remarked on how thoughtful the discussion had been. The concern had been raised. It had been addressed. The decision was documented. Work continued.

Weeks later, when the vulnerability became more pronounced, options were limited. The system had moved past the point where pausing was feasible without significant disruption. Contracts were in place. Timelines were public. Dependencies had multiplied. The question was no longer whether to continue, but how to absorb the impact.

In retrospect, there had been a clear moment when stopping was still possible.

At the time, it did not feel like that moment.

Speed creates this illusion.

The illusion that there will always be another chance to reconsider. Another review. Another gate. Another opportunity to intervene. In practice, those moments diminish as motion accelerates. Each step forward makes the next pause harder.

This is not because people lack courage. It is because systems reward continuation and penalize interruption.

In fast environments, stopping is interpreted as failure of planning rather than as responsible adjustment. It raises questions about competence. It threatens credibility. It introduces uncertainty into narratives that depend on confidence.

As a result, teams learn to delay stopping until it is no longer possible.

This learning is subtle. It is reinforced through experience rather than instruction. People watch what happens when others slow things down. They notice which behaviors are praised and which ones are quietly sidelined. Over time, they internalize the lesson.

The system does not need to silence them. It teaches them when silence is prudent.

Speed also alters how risk is perceived.

Early risks feel abstract. They are discussed in probabilistic terms. They are something to be managed. As work progresses, risks become operational. They are embedded in schedules, contracts, and expectations. At that point, acknowledging them carries cost.

The language shifts accordingly.

What was once described as uncertainty becomes described as volatility. What was once a decision becomes a constraint. What was once an option becomes an assumption. Each shift makes reversal less likely.

Governance mechanisms often reinforce this pattern unintentionally.

Checkpoints are designed to ensure progress, not to question direction. Reviews focus on status rather than substance. Metrics track delivery rather than deliberation. By the time a concern reaches formal oversight, the system is already invested in continuation.

This is why speed is so difficult to confront.

Alignment narrows what can be said. Speed narrows when it can be said. In fast systems, even accurate concerns arrive late. Once motion is underway, timing becomes a form of permission. People learn to keep doubts to themselves not because they lack conviction, but because they understand when conviction will be treated as disruption.

It is not just a preference. It is embedded in structure, incentives, and narrative. It shapes what questions can be asked and when. It defines what counts as professionalism. It determines which decisions feel available.

Once speed dominates, even well-intentioned teams lose the capacity to pause.

This is not a failure of discipline. It is a failure of design.

Teams are rarely given explicit authority to stop work once it has begun. They are given responsibility to deliver. They are measured on progress. They are rewarded for momentum. Under these conditions, continuation becomes the safest choice.

Stopping becomes an exception that must be justified.

This inversion is one of the most powerful ways systems decide before people do.

By the time a leader is asked to approve continuation, the decision has often already been made. The work is in motion. The costs of stopping are visible and immediate. The costs of continuing are distant and uncertain. Under pressure, the system chooses what it can see.

This is why leadership intervention often comes too late.

Leaders inherit decisions that have already crossed the threshold of reversibility. They are asked to manage consequences rather than to choose direction. When outcomes fail, they are blamed for decisions that were structurally constrained long before they were formally endorsed.

Speed makes this pattern feel unavoidable. In reality, it is produced.

Organizations can be designed to preserve pause. They can distinguish between movement and decision. They can create protected spaces where stopping is legitimate even after work has begun.

Most do not.

They equate decisiveness with competence and hesitation with weakness. They celebrate execution and treat reflection as a luxury. They assume that speed is a neutral response to external pressure rather than a design choice with internal consequences.

This assumption is rarely examined.

The result is a system that moves efficiently until it cannot change direction.

When failure becomes visible, it is described as sudden. In fact, it was the predictable outcome of a process that gradually eliminated the option to stop.

Speed did not cause the failure.

It made it irreversible.

What disappears first in fast systems is not intelligence or intent. It is reversibility.

Reversibility is a design property. It is the capacity of a system to pause or change direction before commitment hardens into identity. When reversibility is lost, decisions do not fail because they were wrong, but because they could no longer be undone.

Systems that preserve reversibility protect something else that is rarely named: pause.

Pause is not the absence of action. It is a protected capacity to interrupt motion without reputational penalty once work is underway. Where pause is unprotected, speed becomes non-negotiable, and continuation becomes the safest choice regardless of consequence.

Organizations do not usually decide to eliminate these capacities. They allow them to erode under pressure. What follows is not recklessness, but inevitability.

This chapter is not an argument for slowness. It is an argument for preserving choice.

Regenerative teams are not slow. They are deliberate about where motion begins and where it must remain interruptible. They recognize that the ability to pause is not a matter of willpower, but of design. They protect moments of reversibility explicitly, knowing that speed will otherwise consume them.

Most teams are not built this way. They are built to move, adapt, and deliver. Under sustained pressure, those strengths become liabilities.

The next chapter examines how this pressure reshapes what people are willing to say, and why silence emerges not from fear, but from professionalism learned in fast systems.

Chapter 4
How Silence Is Learned

Silence is usually explained as fear.

People are afraid to speak up. Afraid of retaliation. Afraid of being seen as difficult. Afraid of losing influence or credibility. Leadership literature treats silence as a personal failing, something to be overcome through bravery, psychological safety, or encouragement from above.

This explanation is comforting.

It allows organizations to believe that if people are quiet, it is because they lack courage or trust. It frames silence as a deficit in individuals rather than as an outcome of design. It preserves the belief that if the right conditions were created, people would naturally speak.

That belief is incomplete.

In most organizations, silence is not the absence of voice. It is the result of learning when voice is useful and when it is not. People do not become quiet because they are afraid. They become quiet because they are paying attention.

Silence is a skill. I didn't recognize this as silence at the time; I thought it was maturity.

It is learned through experience. It is reinforced through feedback. It is rewarded in subtle ways that rarely appear in formal guidance. Over time, people internalize when speaking contributes to progress and when it disrupts it. They learn the difference between raising an issue and reopening a decision. They learn how timing shapes legitimacy.

This learning does not require intimidation. It does not require punishment. It requires consistency.

Most organizations provide that consistency.

Early in work, questions are welcomed. Concerns are invited. Alternative perspectives are encouraged. Leaders signal openness. Teams debate. This phase is often described as healthy.

Later, the same questions are received differently.

The work is underway. Decisions have been made. Timelines are in place. Dependencies exist. At this point, raising concerns does not signal diligence. It signals friction. The system responds accordingly.

No one needs to say "don't bring this up." The response is felt. The question is acknowledged, then reframed. The concern is noted, then deprioritized. The discussion moves on.

The person who spoke learns something important.

They learn not that they were wrong, but that they were late.

Silence emerges from this realization.

Once speed dominates and alignment has been reached, timing becomes a form of permission. The same concern expressed earlier would have been welcomed. Expressed now, it threatens progress. People learn to distinguish between those moments quickly.

This is not cowardice. It is competence.

People who remain vocal in these environments are often described as lacking judgment. They are told they do not read the room. They are seen as disruptive, even when they are correct. Over time, organizations sort for those who know when not to speak.

Silence becomes a marker of professionalism.

This is why silence persists even in organizations that value openness. It persists even where leaders genuinely invite feedback. It persists even when no retaliation occurs.

Because the cost is not punishment. It is irrelevance.

Speaking at the wrong time does not get you fired. It gets you bypassed. It reduces your influence. It signals that you do not understand how things work here.

People adapt.

They learn to save their concerns for private conversations. They soften language. They phrase objections as questions. They defer. They wait. Often, they wait too long.

By the time the concern feels urgent enough to raise despite the cost, the system is no longer able to respond.

Silence is not enforced. It is trained.

The Question That Arrived Too Late

The decision had already settled.

Not formally, not yet, but everyone in the room could feel it. The presentation had landed well. The framing was clean. The risks were familiar. The next steps were already appearing on the screen.

As the discussion opened, the questions followed the expected pattern. Clarifications. Confirmations. Small adjustments to scope and sequencing. The conversation moved smoothly, with the quiet confidence that comes when a group believes it is nearing closure.

Near the end, someone spoke.

They did not challenge the recommendation. They did not dispute the analysis. They pointed to an implication that had not been named. It was not a flaw in the plan, but a consequence of it. Something that would not appear immediately, but would matter once execution began.

The room paused.

The response was calm and measured. The implication was acknowledged. Someone explained how it fit within an existing assumption. Another suggested it could be monitored. The language was reassuring. The answer made sense.

Then the conversation moved on.

No one pushed back. No one asked a follow-up. The question did not change the direction of the meeting, but it changed its temperature. The sense of convergence returned, slightly tightened.

When the meeting ended, the decision stood.

Afterward, the person who had spoken replayed the exchange. Not with regret, exactly, but with clarity. They could see the moment more sharply now. The question had been accurate. It had also been late.

They understood what they had misjudged.

It was not the substance of the concern. It was the timing. The decision was no longer open in the way the agenda suggested it was. Raising the implication had not been wrong. It had simply arrived after the system had moved on.

Next time, they would know.

They would raise similar concerns earlier. Or privately. Or not at all.

Nothing about this lesson felt punitive. No one had corrected them. No one had signaled disapproval. The meeting had remained professional throughout.

And yet, something had been learned.

Silence is reinforced not through suppression, but through pattern.

People notice which contributions change outcomes and which ones merely slow them. They notice which concerns are absorbed and which ones alter direction. They learn that raising an issue does not guarantee it will be addressed. They learn that timing matters more than accuracy.

This learning accumulates.

Over time, people internalize the boundaries of acceptable speech. They know which questions belong in early phases and which ones are no longer welcome once motion is underway. They know when disagreement is productive and when it is perceived as resistance.

This knowledge becomes tacit. It is rarely articulated. It is carried in tone, posture, and pacing.

Silence becomes the default response to late insight.

Organizations often misinterpret this silence.

They assume people have nothing to say. They assume concerns would surface if they were serious. They assume the absence of objection indicates agreement.

This assumption is dangerous.

Silence does not mean consensus. It means calculation.

People are constantly weighing the value of speaking against the likelihood of effect. When systems reward momentum, the calculation shifts. Speaking becomes less about truth and more about timing. Concerns that cannot be acted upon are withheld. Observations that disrupt flow are deferred.

Eventually, people stop raising issues that fall outside the narrow window of influence.

This is how silence becomes systemic.

It does not require fear. It requires predictability.

Once people can predict that speaking late will change nothing and cost something, silence becomes rational.

This is why exhortations to "speak up" so often fail. They ignore the structure that makes speaking ineffective. They place responsibility back on individuals while leaving the conditions untouched.

Telling people to be brave in systems that punish interruption is not empowerment. It is displacement.

Silence also changes how organizations understand themselves.

When concerns are filtered before they reach formal channels, leaders receive a sanitized picture of reality. Information arrives already shaped to fit what the system can absorb. What remains unsaid is invisible, even to those who would genuinely want to hear it.

This creates a feedback gap.

Leaders interpret silence as alignment. They assume absence of objection equals support. They move forward with confidence. Later, when consequences surface, they are surprised by issues they were never told about.

This surprise is often framed as failure of communication.

In reality, it is failure of timing.

The system made it difficult to speak when speaking could still matter.

Silence protects individuals in the short term. It protects organizations in the long term only superficially.

By the time concerns emerge forcefully enough to be unavoidable, options have collapsed. What could have been addressed through redesign must now be managed through response.

Silence does not prevent failure. It delays its visibility and reshapes identity.

People who learn when not to speak are often promoted. They are seen as politically savvy. They are trusted. They are described as good partners. Over time, the organization selects for those who can navigate its unspoken rules.

This selection reinforces the pattern.

Those who continue to raise uncomfortable issues are labeled as difficult. Those who adapt are rewarded. The system becomes increasingly homogeneous in how it processes information. Diversity of thought narrows, not because it is absent, but because it is filtered out before it reaches decision points.

Silence becomes part of the culture, but it is not cultural in origin.

It is structural.

Once alignment has been reached and speed has taken hold, silence is the natural outcome. It is how people preserve influence. It is how they avoid being seen as obstacles. It is how they continue to function inside systems that value movement over reconsideration.

This is why silence persists even in organizations that invest heavily in psychological safety. Safety does not change the cost of being late. It does not restore the ability to pause. It does not reopen decisions that momentum has already closed.

Silence is not the opposite of engagement. It is engagement constrained by timing.

People are still thinking. They are still noticing. They are still evaluating risk. They are simply no longer sharing everything they see.

This is the moment where complicity becomes personal.

Not because people agree with the direction, but because they continue to participate in its execution knowing that their concerns will no longer be welcomed. Silence allows work to proceed smoothly. It reduces friction. It preserves coherence.

It also allows harm to travel without resistance.

Most people who remain silent do not believe they are doing anything wrong. They tell themselves the issue has been noted. That it can be addressed later. That raising it again would not help. These beliefs are often correct within the system as it exists.

That is precisely the problem.

Silence becomes ethical not because it is right, but because the system makes alternatives impractical.

This is how good people find themselves implementing decisions they no longer fully support.

This chapter is not a call for more speaking.

It is a recognition that silence is learned because speaking is constrained.

Regenerative teams do not rely on courage to overcome silence. They redesign timing. They create protected moments where late insights can still interrupt motion without penalty. They distinguish between expression and influence. They ensure that raising concerns does not depend on perfect timing to be effective.

Most teams do not do this.

They assume silence reflects comfort or agreement. They mistake professionalism for alignment. They believe that if something mattered enough, someone would say something.

This belief is another form of the ancient error.

It treats silence as personal choice rather than as structural adaptation.

The next chapter examines where the cost of this adaptation lands, and why teams themselves become the place where unresolved tension is absorbed, carried, and eventually normalized.

Chapter 5

Teams as Shock Absorbers

Teams are rarely asked to absorb contradiction.

They are expected to deliver outcomes, coordinate effort, and solve problems. They are given goals, timelines, and constraints. They are praised for collaboration and adaptability. When work becomes difficult, teams are encouraged to be resilient, to lean in, to find a way.

What is rarely acknowledged is that teams are also where unresolved tension goes to hide.

When systems simplify decisions too early, when momentum overrides judgment, and when silence becomes professional competence, the work does not stop. It continues. But it continues with gaps. With inconsistencies. With consequences that no longer have a clear owner.

Those consequences land in teams.

Teams become the place where incompatible demands are reconciled. Where strategic ambiguity is translated into operational reality. Where ethical discomfort is managed quietly so work can proceed. They do this not because they are asked to, but because they are closest to the work and farthest from the authority to refuse it.

This is not failure. I used to describe teams like this as resilient, before I understood what they were actually being asked to do. In reality, it is absorption.

Organizations rely on this absorption more than they admit. It allows systems to appear coherent at the top while remaining flexible at the edges. It allows leaders to move forward without resolving every tension explicitly. It allows plans to survive contact with reality.

The cost of that survival is rarely tracked.

Teams learn to bridge gaps informally. They create workarounds. They make tradeoffs no one authorized but everyone depends on. They smooth contradictions between priorities that were never reconciled. They take on emotional and cognitive labor that does not appear in project plans or performance metrics.

From the outside, this looks like competence.

From the inside, it feels like carrying something that was never meant to be yours.

Over time, this absorption becomes normal. Teams stop expecting clarity. They stop asking for resolution. They assume that strain is part of the job. They internalize the belief that if something feels impossible, they simply have not worked hard enough yet.

This is where systems succeed by offloading their own unresolved decisions.

The next section examines how this offloading happens quietly, why it is rewarded, and how teams come to mistake absorption for professionalism.

Unresolved tension does not disappear.

When decisions are simplified too early, when speed removes the ability to pause, and when silence becomes the competent response, the work still has to happen. Commitments still have to be met. Consequences still have to be managed. The system does not stop because judgment was deferred.

It relocates the cost.

Teams are the most convenient place for that cost to go.

They are close enough to the work to see what is breaking. They are skilled enough to improvise around it. They are invested enough to care about outcomes. And they are distant enough from formal authority that absorbing contradiction feels like part of the job rather than a decision that requires consent.

This is why teams become the default container for what the system cannot resolve.

No one assigns this role explicitly. It emerges naturally from structure. When ambiguity flows downward faster than authority flows upward, teams compensate. They translate strategic uncertainty into operational action. They reconcile incompatible priorities through effort rather than escalation. They make decisions in the gaps left by governance, often without realizing that they are doing so.

From the outside, this looks like adaptability.

From the inside, it feels like carrying something heavier than what was agreed.

Teams learn to bridge contradictions informally. They create workarounds that allow delivery to continue. They take on additional coordination, additional emotional labor, additional risk. They smooth over inconsistencies between what was promised and what is possible.

They do this quietly.

They do it because stopping would require explanation. Because escalation would require authority they do not have. Because failure would land on them anyway. Over time, absorption becomes the path of least resistance.

This is not resilience. It is displacement.

The Work That Was Never Assigned

The team had a reputation for reliability.

They were known for delivering under pressure, for navigating complexity without complaint, for finding solutions where others stalled. When plans ran into trouble, leadership trusted them to figure it out. That trust felt earned. It also carried weight.

The issue they faced was not a single problem. It was a set of small inconsistencies that, taken together, made the work harder than it should have been. Requirements conflicted. Timelines overlapped in unrealistic ways. Stakeholder expectations had not been fully aligned upstream.

None of this was new. Each issue had been noted somewhere. Each had a reasonable explanation. None, on its own, rose to the level that justified stopping the work.

So the team adjusted.

They re-sequenced tasks. They absorbed delays by extending their own hours. They negotiated compromises between stakeholders who never met each other directly. They made judgment calls to keep things moving, even when those calls carried risk.

No one told them to do this.

They did it because the alternative was visible failure.

As the work progressed, the team became increasingly central to the project's success. They were the ones who understood how the pieces actually fit together. They were the ones who knew where the gaps were. They were the ones who could anticipate issues before they surfaced.

Leadership praised their performance. Their adaptability was cited as a strength. Their ability to "own the work" was held up as an example for others.

What was not acknowledged was that the team was now carrying decisions that had never been resolved.

They were absorbing the consequences of tradeoffs made elsewhere. They were managing tensions that should have been reconciled at a higher level. They were doing invisible work to preserve coherence.

When the project succeeded, the team was congratulated.

When it struggled, the pressure intensified.

At no point did anyone ask whether this load belonged to them.

Teams often experience this absorption as professionalism.

They take pride in being the group that can handle complexity. They value their ability to make things work despite imperfect conditions. They develop shared norms around stepping in, staying late, and protecting the work from external disruption.

These norms are rarely questioned because they are rewarded.

Performance reviews praise flexibility. Leaders express appreciation for dedication. The organization signals that this is what competence looks like. Over time, teams internalize the belief that absorbing strain is part of their role.

This belief is dangerous.

It trains teams to treat structural problems as personal challenges. It reframes design failures as opportunities for heroics. It encourages people to solve problems that should have been escalated or redesigned.

As this pattern repeats, the team's identity shifts.

What began as a response to temporary conditions becomes a permanent mode of operation. The team no longer expects clarity. They assume contradiction. They stop asking whether a demand makes sense and focus instead on how to accommodate it.

This is how overload becomes normal.

Burnout is often the first visible symptom, but it is not the core issue. Burnout signals that absorption has exceeded capacity, not that the team lacks resilience. Moral injury appears alongside it, as people are asked to implement decisions that conflict with their judgment but feel unavoidable given their position.

Teams rarely name this injury. They experience it as frustration, fatigue, or disengagement. They tell themselves that the pressure is temporary, that the next project will be different, that this is just how work is right now.

The system benefits from this normalization.

As long as teams continue to absorb contradiction, the system is able to continue without paying for it. Plans can remain intact. Difficult tradeoffs can remain implicit rather than explicit.

Teams become shock absorbers.

They protect the system from the consequences of its own unresolved decisions by taking those consequences into themselves.

This absorption has limits.

As teams carry more and more unresolved tension, their ability to adapt erodes. Workarounds become brittle. Informal coordination breaks down. People leave, taking with them the tacit knowledge that made absorption possible.

When failure finally becomes visible, it is often framed as a breakdown at the team level.

The team burned out.
The team could not handle the load.
The team lost focus.

These explanations preserve the illusion that the system itself remains sound.

What is rarely acknowledged is that the team failed because it succeeded for too long at absorbing what should never have been theirs.

This is where the cost of silence and speed converges.

Silence allows contradictions to pass downward unchallenged. Speed prevents those contradictions from being resolved before they harden. Teams absorb what remains so the system can continue to function.

By the time leaders see the effects, the damage has already occurred.

This is why calls for resilience feel hollow to people inside these teams. They are being asked to endure the consequences of decisions they did not make and cannot change. Strength becomes a liability. Adaptability becomes a trap.

The more capable the team, the more they are relied upon to absorb.

This reliance is not accidental. It is structural.

Organizations optimize for continuity. Teams provide it.

Chapter 5 does not end with blame.

Teams do not choose to become shock absorbers in a meaningful sense. They adapt to the conditions they are given. They do what competent, committed people do when faced with incompatible demands and insufficient authority.

The problem is not that teams absorb tension.

The problem is that systems rely on this absorption without acknowledging its cost.

As long as teams continue to make contradictions workable, the need for redesign remains invisible. Success masks fragility. Delivery conceals damage.

The next chapter examines how this hidden load shapes roles, accountability, and authority, and why organizations come to depend on people who can carry more than they should.

Chapter 6
Authority Without Control

Authority is assumed to confer control.

Organizations are built around this assumption. Titles, reporting lines, approval gates, and accountability frameworks all rest on the belief that those who hold authority can meaningfully influence outcomes. When something goes wrong, we look to the person in charge and ask why they did not intervene.

Increasingly, that question has no honest answer.

In modern organizations, authority often arrives too late to matter.

Decisions are framed, constrained, and effectively settled long before they reach formal approval. By the time a leader is asked to decide, the range of available options has already narrowed. Dependencies are fixed. Commitments have been made. Reversal would carry visible cost, while continuation feels responsible.

Authority remains visible. Control does not. I have sat in that position, asked to approve something that was already socially impossible to stop, and understood exactly why saying no would change nothing.

This is not a failure of leadership character or competence. It is the result of how contemporary systems sequence decision making under pressure.

Speed, alignment, silence, and absorption all work together to move judgment earlier and consequence later. Authority appears at the end of this process, not the beginning.

When authority is exercised after choice has collapsed, it changes function.

Approval becomes endorsement rather than selection. Oversight becomes confirmation rather than interrogation. Accountability becomes retrospective rather than preventative. Leaders are asked to stand behind decisions they did not meaningfully shape, and to absorb consequences they could no longer avoid.

This is why leadership feels heavier even as formal power expands.

Leaders are expected to take responsibility for outcomes produced by systems that no longer allow them to intervene at the point where it would matter. They are judged on results without being given access to the moments where those results were decided.

Authority without control is not symbolic. It is punitive.

Boards and executives are assumed to be the final line of defense.

They are charged with oversight. They approve strategy. They are accountable for outcomes that affect shareholders, employees, communities, and ecosystems. When failure occurs, they are asked why they allowed it to happen.

The assumption beneath this questioning is simple. If authority exists at the top, then control must exist there as well.

Increasingly, that assumption is false.

In many modern organizations, boards and executives retain formal authority while losing practical control over the conditions that produce failure. They approve decisions whose consequences have already been shaped elsewhere. They are presented with options that differ only in degree, not in kind. They are asked to choose between versions of continuation.

By the time a decision reaches the boardroom, the system has often already decided.

This does not happen because boards are inattentive or executives are weak. It happens because governance has been redesigned, intentionally or not, to operate after momentum has hardened rather than before judgment is required.

Board agendas are structured around progress updates, risk summaries, and assurance statements. These materials are prepared weeks in advance. They reflect decisions already embedded in contracts, timelines, and public commitments. They arrive polished, coherent, and difficult to interrupt without appearing irresponsible.

The board's role becomes confirmatory.

This shift is subtle, but profound. Oversight moves from shaping direction to validating motion. The question is no longer "should we proceed?" but "are we comfortable with how this is proceeding?" Those are not the same questions. One preserves choice. The other manages exposure.

Executives experience the same narrowing, often earlier.

As organizations scale, executives become dependent on layers of interpretation. Information is summarized, filtered, and framed long before it reaches them. What arrives are dashboards, narratives, and risk ratings that have already translated complexity into manageable form. The system does this efficiently. It has to.

What it cannot do is surface what no longer fits.

Late-stage risks, interaction effects, and second-order consequences are rarely presented as decisions. They are presented as conditions to be managed. By the time an executive sees them, the organization is already committed to a course of action.

Authority remains, but the moment of choice has passed.

This is why board interventions increasingly feel reactive rather than preventative. When boards push back, they are told that reversal would be costly. When they ask for alternatives, they are shown scenarios that preserve the same trajectory. When they express concern, they are reassured by controls designed to manage fallout rather than avoid it.

The board is not powerless. But it is constrained by timing.

This constraint reshapes behavior at the top.

Executives learn which battles can still be fought and which ones cannot. Boards learn where pressure will be absorbed and where it will rebound. Over time, both adapt. They focus on monitoring rather than interrupting. They ask better questions within the frame they are given, rather than questioning the frame itself.

This adaptation is rational.

Boards are judged on stability. Executives are judged on continuity. Both are rewarded for avoiding disruption. In this environment, insisting on late-stage reversal can appear reckless, even when it is responsible.

Authority becomes risk management.

The Approval That Could Not Be Withheld

The board had concerns.

They were not new concerns. They had been raised in earlier discussions, noted in committee minutes, and flagged in risk summaries. None of them were trivial. None of them had stopped the work.

The proposal on the agenda was presented as a continuation, not a decision. Contracts were in place. External commitments had been made. Reputational exposure was real. Delaying now would require explanation to investors, partners, and regulators.

Management presented options.

Each option assumed forward motion. The differences were in sequencing, not direction. Mitigations were outlined. Contingencies were described. The risks were categorized and rated.

The board asked questions.

They asked whether the assumptions still held. They asked about downside exposure. They asked how success would be measured. The answers were thorough. The material was sound.

At one point, a director asked what it would take to stop.

The room paused.

Stopping was discussed briefly. The cost was summarized. Financial impact. Market perception. Internal disruption. The message was clear, though no one stated it directly. Stopping was technically possible. It was no longer plausible.

The board voted to approve.

The decision was unanimous.

After the meeting, several directors expressed unease privately. Not about the process, which had been proper, but about the outcome, which felt constrained. They had exercised their authority. They had also recognized its limits.

Later, when the initiative failed to deliver as expected, the board was criticized for approving it. Questions were asked about oversight. Investigations focused on governance failures.

The moment when stopping had still been possible did not appear in the record.

Boards and executives are increasingly asked to absorb blame for decisions they no longer meaningfully control.

This is the inversion at the heart of modern governance.

Accountability concentrates upward. Control disperses outward and downward. Teams absorb operational contradiction. Executives absorb consequence. Boards absorb legitimacy risk. Everyone carries something they did not choose.

This arrangement is unstable.

It produces burnout at the top that mirrors burnout at the edges. Executives describe feeling trapped between expectations and constraints they cannot reconcile. Board members describe being asked to take responsibility for outcomes shaped by forces outside their direct influence.

When authority cannot interrupt momentum, it becomes symbolic.

Symbolic authority is dangerous because it preserves the appearance of control while eroding its substance. It reassures stakeholders that someone is in charge, even when the system no longer allows that person to decide.

This is why replacing leaders feels like resolution.

It restores the symbol.

What it does not restore is control.

Each cycle of replacement reinforces the illusion that authority remains intact, while leaving untouched the structural conditions that hollowed it out. Boards approve new leaders with renewed confidence. Executives arrive with mandate and resolve. The system continues to decide early.

The new leader inherits the same timing problem.

This is not a call for stronger boards or tougher executives. Strength is not the missing variable.

The missing variable is authority exercised at the right moment.

Until boards and executives regain the ability to interrupt motion before commitments harden, governance will remain retrospective. Oversight will focus on managing damage rather than preventing it. Accountability will continue to function as punishment rather than protection.

Authority without control is not leadership. It is exposure.

This chapter does not argue that boards and executives are irrelevant.

It argues that they are being placed in an impossible position.

They are asked to guarantee outcomes without access to the moments where outcomes are decided. They are held accountable for decisions that arrive framed, constrained, and difficult to refuse. They are expected to intervene after momentum has become identity.

This is not a failure of will. It is a failure of design.

The chapters that follow examine how roles, authority, and accountability must be re-anchored if regeneration is to be more than a moral aspiration. They ask what it would take for authority to matter again, not in title or blame, but in timing.

Until that question is faced honestly, boards will continue to approve what they cannot stop, executives will continue to manage consequences they cannot prevent, and teams will continue to absorb what no one else will carry.

That is not governance.

It is displacement at scale.

Chapter 7
When Roles Collapse and Accountability Distorts

Modern organizations rely on roles.

Roles define authority, responsibility, scope, and expectation. They are meant to create clarity. They are meant to distribute work rationally. They are meant to ensure that decisions are made at appropriate levels and that accountability follows authority.

In practice, roles rarely remain intact under pressure.

They compress.

As systems accelerate, simplify, and defer judgment, the boundaries that once separated decision making, execution, and accountability begin to blur. Work does not disappear when roles become unclear. It moves. It accumulates. It concentrates.

Most often, it concentrates in the middle.

Managers, sponsors, product owners, portfolio leads, and functional heads are asked to reconcile demands that were never designed to coexist. They are given responsibility for outcomes without control over inputs. They are expected to deliver certainty downstream while absorbing uncertainty from above.

This is not role failure. It is role distortion.

The Myth of the Clear Role

Organizations talk constantly about role clarity.

Job descriptions are written. RACI charts are produced. Governance models are documented. On paper, responsibilities are well defined. In reality, clarity collapses the moment pressure rises.

When alignment is reached early, when speed becomes non-negotiable, and when silence becomes competence, the system no longer respects role boundaries. Decisions are made implicitly, commitments are assumed, and work is already underway by the time formal responsibility is invoked.

Roles adapt accordingly.

People begin doing what needs to be done rather than what their role formally authorizes. They fill gaps. They translate vague direction into concrete action. They make tradeoffs without mandate because someone has to.

This adaptation is praised.

Organizations reward those who "step up," who "own the outcome," who "act like leaders regardless of title." These phrases sound empowering. They are also signals that role boundaries have failed.

The moment an organization celebrates boundary crossing as virtue, it has stopped protecting roles as design instruments.

Accountability Without Control

Role compression produces a specific and damaging distortion.

Accountability remains explicit.
Control becomes implicit.

Managers are held accountable for delivery while being constrained by decisions made elsewhere. Sponsors are accountable for outcomes while being excluded from early judgment. Portfolio leads are accountable for performance while inheriting commitments they did not shape.

This mismatch is rarely acknowledged directly.

Instead, it is reframed as leadership expectation. People are told that seniority requires dealing with ambiguity, that maturity involves working with imperfect information, that responsibility includes adapting to constraints.

There is truth in this.

There is also a limit.

When accountability consistently exceeds control, roles stop functioning as stabilizers and begin functioning as stress concentrators.

The system relies on this concentration.

It allows strategic ambiguity to persist while operational certainty is demanded. It allows decisions to remain unresolved at the top while delivery is enforced below. It allows governance to appear intact while authority fragments in practice.

Role compression is how this contradiction is managed.

The Manager as Translator

In compressed systems, middle roles do not simply execute decisions. They translate them.

This translation is rarely acknowledged as work. It is treated as judgment, initiative, or leadership instinct. In reality, it is the mechanism by which unresolved tension is converted into action without ever being formally resolved.

Managers translate strategy into delivery even when strategy is incomplete. They translate competing priorities into schedules that appear coherent. They translate executive confidence into operational urgency. They translate risk language into task language. Each translation makes the system move.

This translation is not neutral.

Every act of translation simplifies. It removes ambiguity. It resolves conflict. It selects one interpretation over another.

In doing so, it quietly eliminates alternatives that were never explicitly rejected. What survives translation is what can be acted on. What does not fit is set aside.

The system benefits from this elimination.

By the time work reaches execution, it appears orderly. Tradeoffs have been made, but they are no longer visible as tradeoffs. They appear as constraints. What was once a question becomes a condition. What was once a disagreement becomes a dependency.

Managers do not do this because they want power. They do it because refusing to translate would stall the system. Escalating every ambiguity would overwhelm governance. Waiting for clarity would be interpreted as inability to lead.

So they translate.

Over time, this becomes the role's defining competence.

Good managers are not those who surface contradiction. They are those who absorb it and make it workable. They are praised for decisiveness, pragmatism, and ownership. Their success is measured by continuity, not by the quality of the judgments they were forced to make in the gaps.

This is how translation replaces decision making without anyone naming it as such.

What disappears in this process is not disagreement, but accountability for the choices embedded in translation. When outcomes fail, the system rarely asks which contradictions were resolved informally or which alternatives were never escalated. It asks why execution fell short.

The translator becomes the accountable party.

The Work That Cannot Be Named

As roles compress, a category of work emerges that cannot be easily named or tracked.

It does not appear in project plans or budgets. It is not captured in role descriptions. It is not discussed openly in governance forums. Yet it is essential to keeping the system functioning.

This work includes negotiating between stakeholders whose priorities were never reconciled. It includes absorbing downstream fallout from upstream decisions that arrived already committed. It includes protecting teams from shifting direction while enforcing unrealistic timelines. It includes maintaining morale while delivering outcomes that feel increasingly disconnected from purpose. It includes carrying ethical discomfort without authority to change direction.

This work is invisible by necessity.

If it were named, it would reveal the contradictions the system prefers to keep implicit. It would expose where decisions were deferred rather than made. It would force questions about authority, sequencing, and refusal that the organization is not prepared to answer.

So the work remains unnamed.

Because it is unnamed, it cannot be resourced. Because it cannot be resourced, it is absorbed through effort. Because it is absorbed through effort, it becomes normalized. And because it is normalized, it is expected.

This is how invisible work becomes structural dependency.

The system comes to rely on people who can perform this work without recognition. It rewards them quietly through trust, access, and advancement. It treats their capacity to absorb as a personal strength rather than as a compensatory mechanism for design failure.

Over time, those who cannot or will not perform this invisible work are filtered out. They are described as inflexible, not strategic, not ready. The organization selects for those willing to carry more than their role formally authorizes.

This selection process is rarely intentional. It emerges from repeated patterns of reward and neglect. But its effect is profound. It reshapes who remains, who rises, and what kinds of judgment survive inside the system.

The work that cannot be named becomes the work that holds everything together.

The Cost of Being "Reasonable"

People in compressed roles learn quickly what is expected of them.

They learn that escalation is risky.
They learn that refusal is punished.
They learn that asking for clarity can be interpreted as incompetence.
They learn that being "reasonable" means making things work.

This learning is reinforced through subtle feedback.

Those who push back are labeled difficult.
Those who comply are trusted.
Those who absorb are promoted.

The organization selects for people who can carry contradiction quietly.

Over time, this selection reshapes the organization's leadership pipeline.

Those who rise are not necessarily those with the best judgment.
They are those most willing and able to reconcile impossible demands without exposing the underlying design failure.

This is how organizations institutionalize role distortion.

When Accountability Becomes Personal

Role compression also reshapes how people experience responsibility.

When outcomes fail, accountability rarely traces back to the conditions that made failure likely. It concentrates on the role closest to execution.

Managers are asked why they did not foresee the issue.
Sponsors are asked why they did not intervene.
Portfolio leads are asked why they did not adjust priorities.

Each of these questions assumes control that no longer existed.

People internalize this failure.

They replay decisions.
They question their judgment.
They take on responsibility for outcomes they could not have prevented.

This is where moral injury deepens.

Not because people acted unethically, but because they were placed in roles where acting ethically would have required refusing work they were not permitted to refuse.

The Illusion of Empowerment

Organizations often describe role compression as empowerment.

Managers are given ownership. Teams are trusted to decide. Roles are expanded. Autonomy is celebrated. On the surface, this language signals respect and confidence. Beneath it, a different shift is taking place.

What is being expanded is not authority. It is exposure.

People are asked to make decisions without protection. They are held accountable without control. They are praised for autonomy while being constrained by commitments they did not shape and cannot refuse.

This is not empowerment. It is displacement.

Calling it empowerment allows the system to remain clean. It reframes the transfer of unresolved tension as a gift rather than a burden. It converts structural abdication into personal growth. It allows leadership to appear generous while leaving the underlying design untouched.

Ownership, in this context, does not mean owning the decision. It means owning the consequences.

When outcomes succeed, the system credits adaptability. When they fail, it questions judgment. In neither case does it revisit the conditions that made those outcomes likely.

This is why empowerment rhetoric feels hollow to people inside compressed roles. They recognize that what they have been given is responsibility without the right to refuse, adapt without the ability to stop, and autonomy without insulation from risk.

Exposure masquerades as trust.

The system depends on this confusion. As long as people accept expanded exposure as empowerment, role distortion can persist without challenge. The language reassures everyone involved while the cost continues to accumulate.

The Breaking Point

Role compression can persist for long periods without visible failure.

As long as capable people continue to absorb contradiction, the system appears to function. Performance metrics hold. Delivery continues. Issues are managed informally. From the outside, the organization looks resilient.

This apparent stability is misleading.

What is actually happening is that failure thresholds are being displaced rather than reduced. Risk is not removed. It is carried forward by people who are compensating for unresolved design choices. The system remains intact because those compensations are effective, not because the underlying conditions are sound.

Over time, this creates a dangerous illusion of durability.

Because problems are being managed rather than resolved, leadership receives fewer signals that redesign is necessary. Governance sees execution rather than strain. What looks like adaptability is often exhaustion operating below the threshold of visibility.

The breaking point does not arrive because people suddenly stop coping.

It arrives because the conditions that require coping remain unchanged while capacity quietly erodes.

As role compression continues, the informal workarounds that once held the system together become brittle. Judgment shortcuts accumulate. Ethical compromises that once felt temporary begin to feel normal. People stop questioning demands not because they agree with them, but because questioning no longer changes outcomes.

At this stage, failure is no longer an anomaly. It is latent.

When it finally surfaces, it often appears disproportionate to the triggering event. A missed deadline, a regulatory breach, a reputational incident, or a sudden wave of attrition is treated as the cause. In reality, it is merely the point at which accumulated strain can no longer be absorbed.

This is why postmortems so often focus on proximate errors rather than structural conditions. By the time failure is visible, the roles that could have surfaced the contradiction earlier are already exhausted, exited, or discredited.

The system does not fail because roles were unclear.

It fails because roles were used to carry decisions the system refused to make.

Why This Matters for Regeneration

Regenerative systems actively hold tension at the level where it can still be shaped.

They distribute authority in ways that allow difficult decisions to surface early, before commitment hardens into identity. They design roles so that judgment is exercised upstream of delivery, not displaced into execution. They treat escalation as a normal function of system health, not as a personal failure of nerve or competence.

In such systems, roles remain intact under pressure.

Responsibility does not migrate faster than control. Translation does not replace decision. Absorption is not mistaken for capability. When contradictions arise, they are addressed explicitly rather than managed through effort and endurance.

This is how regeneration becomes structural rather than rhetorical.

People are not praised for coping with overload. They are protected from carrying decisions they did not make and cannot change. Systems remain responsive because they do not rely on sacrifice to maintain coherence. When failure occurs, it is traced back to conditions and choices, not assigned to roles that were never given the authority to refuse.

Refining role descriptions or updating competency models will not fix this. Roles only become coherent again when the system stops asking them to carry contradictions they did not create. In regenerative systems, clarity emerges from design integrity, not documentation.

Roles are constructed to carry the weight they are authorized to bear. Accountability is matched by real control, exercised early enough to preserve choice. Translation is visible, shared, and bounded, rather than hidden inside individual effort.

Under these conditions, regeneration is not an aspiration. It is a property of how the system functions.

The chapters that follow examine how organizations begin to create these conditions, not by asking people to do more, but by deciding less, earlier, and with greater consequence.

Chapter 8

When Portfolios Decide Before People Do

In project-driven organizations, portfolios exist to allocate funding, sequence work, and manage capacity. They determine which initiatives are approved, which are deferred, and which never begin. They shape staffing decisions, investment horizons, and delivery expectations. They are the mechanism through which strategy becomes commitments that can be staffed, scheduled, and measured.

The portfolio's most consequential act is not prioritization. It is conversion. Portfolios convert intent into obligation. Once a project, program, or product initiative enters the portfolio, its status changes. It is no longer an option competing with alternatives. It becomes funded work, surrounded by budgets, timelines, dependencies, and expectations that transform continuation from a choice into a responsibility.

That transformation matters because it quietly changes what "good governance" looks like inside the system. Early on, governance is framed as decision making. Later, it is framed as delivery assurance. The organization shifts from deciding what should be done to ensuring that what has been approved is delivered. What looks like discipline often becomes persistence.

What looks like accountability often becomes follow-through on a decision whose conditions have already changed.

Stopping is no longer neutral.

In portfolio logic, stopping is treated as failure, waste, or loss of momentum. The organization may still say it values learning, adaptation, and agility, but once commitments harden, the moral status of the decision changes. Continuing feels responsible. Stopping feels like admitting the original approval was wrong, or worse, that the organization is not in control of itself. That is why so many organizations keep moving even when they can see the work no longer makes sense. They are not choosing to be reckless. They are choosing to remain coherent under the logic the portfolio has already set in motion.

Approval as Commitment, Not Choice

Portfolio processes are designed to make selection feel disciplined. Business cases are prepared. Benefits are forecast. Risks are assessed. Stage gates are defined. Approval bodies authorize work. The artifacts are familiar, and the rituals are reassuring. They create the appearance of deliberate choice.

What is less visible is how quickly approval hardens into obligation. Once work is approved, the language around it changes. The initiative becomes "the project." Delivery plans are activated. External commitments may be made. Internal credibility becomes tied to progress. People begin aligning their work, their calendars, and their reputations around the assumption that this initiative is now real and must succeed.

At that stage, stopping requires explanation. Continuing does not.

This is not because anyone has decided that stopping is forbidden. It is because the portfolio has already created a structure in which stopping is costly in ways the system can easily see, while continuing is costly in ways the system can defer. The visible costs are immediate. The schedule impact. The disruption to teams. The messaging required. The perceived loss of discipline. The invisible costs are slower. Compounding risk. Opportunity cost. Moral injury. Degraded trust. Technical debt. Exhausted capacity. By the time those costs become visible, the system has moved on to managing consequences rather than revisiting choice.

This is how reversibility erodes. The organization still holds formal mechanisms for review, but those mechanisms often function as monitoring rather than reconsideration. Reviews focus on status, spend, and delivery confidence. Questions are framed around execution rather than direction. Governance shifts into assurance mode. The underlying decision is treated as settled, and any discomfort is translated into risk management rather than decision revision.

This is where the portfolio stops being a decision space and becomes a commitment engine.

The Myth of the Failing Project

When projects fail, they are rarely described as bad decisions. They are described as execution problems. Scope was unclear. Risks were underestimated. Stakeholders were misaligned. The team lacked capability. The sponsor did not intervene early enough. These explanations are often true in the narrow sense. They are also convenient in a broader one.

Each explanation preserves a critical assumption: that the project itself was still the right choice.

Portfolio logic depends on that assumption. If an organization admits that a project no longer makes sense once new information emerges, it has to confront the limits of its portfolio decision process. It has to accept that approval is conditional, that strategy evolves, and that stopping can be an act of judgment rather than failure. That kind of admission threatens the legitimacy of the approval ritual itself. It implies that the organization cannot reliably convert strategy into commitments that hold.

Most portfolios are not designed to tolerate that implication. They are designed to protect continuity of investment and stability of plan.

As a result, portfolio reviews often function as mechanisms for defending past commitments rather than revisiting them. Risks are reframed as manageable. Deviations are explained. Mitigations are added. The system becomes very good at keeping work alive. The organization treats persistence as proof of seriousness and reversal as evidence of weakness. It may call this discipline. It may call it maturity. In practice, it is often a refusal to reopen a decision once commitment has become identity.

This is not dishonesty. It is portfolio logic operating as intended. The portfolio is doing what it was designed to do: preserve continuity, protect invested effort, and maintain coherence. The problem is that coherence is sometimes purchased by deferring judgment until judgment can no longer change anything.

Change Initiatives and the Illusion of Inevitability

The same dynamic applies to change initiatives and transformation programs. Once a transformation program is approved, it quickly acquires the status of inevitability. Leadership has announced it. Communications are underway. External narratives are in motion. Internal resistance is framed as delivery risk rather than as potential signal. The organization begins treating the transformation not as a hypothesis to test, but as a future to enforce.

At that point, questioning the direction of the change is no longer experienced as judgment. It is experienced as obstruction.

Portfolio tracking reinforces this shift. The initiative is monitored against milestones that assume continuation. Reviews focus on adoption, not reconsideration. The question becomes how to implement the change, not whether it still makes sense given what is being learned. Where learning contradicts the plan, learning is reframed as "change management." It is treated as a problem to be absorbed rather than information that should alter the decision.

The future has already been decided. What remains is managing the consequences.

This is one of the most important ways portfolios decide before people do. They do not simply select work. They create inevitability. They build a structure in which reversal is treated as failure, and so reversal becomes rare even when it is responsible.

How Portfolio Logic Pre-empts Choice

Portfolio decisions are made early, under conditions of optimism and incomplete information. That is not a moral failing. It is a structural reality. The portfolio must make choices before the work is known, because waiting until the work is fully known would mean never starting. The portfolio therefore depends on forecasts, assumptions, and confidence.

The problem is not that portfolios decide early. The problem is what happens after they do.

Once funding is allocated and work is sequenced, the organization begins organizing itself around success. Careers become attached. Reputations form. Metrics align. Dependencies multiply. The cost of stopping increases with every review cycle because stopping is no longer just an economic decision. It becomes a social decision and a legitimacy decision. It asks the organization to admit that it committed prematurely, or that it cannot adapt without appearing unstable.

At this point, sunk cost is not psychological. It is structural. Stopping would require unwinding commitments that now span people, systems, and external relationships. It would require explaining reversal to stakeholders who were told the work was necessary. It would expose the limits of the original decision process. Continuation becomes the path of least resistance, and the organization calls that path responsibility.

This is how portfolios quietly transform uncertainty into inevitability. The initial approval may have been a decision. Everything afterward is often treated as follow-through. The organization confuses persistence with integrity, as if continuing is proof that the original decision was sound. In reality, continuing is often proof that reversibility has been lost.

Where Judgment Is Lost

Portfolios are optimized for throughput, not for reconsideration. They are effective at deciding what comes next. They are far less capable of deciding what should stop. Reprioritization is framed as reshuffling, not refusal. Stopping is treated as exceptional rather than as a normal outcome of learning.

As a result, judgment is exercised almost entirely at the front end. Once work is underway, learning accumulates, but the capacity to act on that learning diminishes. The system becomes backward-looking. It manages variance instead of revisiting assumptions. It explains deviation instead of questioning direction. It treats persistence as virtue and reversal as weakness. This is not because people lack courage. It is because the portfolio has already decided, and the organization has already reorganized itself around that decision.

This is the point where many systems begin confusing progress with motion. Status updates become proof of control. Dashboards become proxies for understanding. Confidence ratings become substitutes for judgment. The portfolio becomes a place where work is tracked, not where the future remains open.

That is why the most important portfolio question is rarely asked: what should we stop?

The absence of that question is not a gap in maturity. It is a design outcome. Most portfolios are not designed to reward stopping. They are designed to punish it, subtly or overtly, because stopping destabilizes the very continuity portfolios exist to protect.

The Consequence for Teams and Leaders

By the time a team experiences a decision as irreversible, it is already absorbing the cost. By the time a sponsor recognizes that the work no longer makes sense, their role has shifted from choice to damage control. By the time senior oversight engages, the tools available are retrospective. Everyone is acting rationally within the structure they inhabit. The structure itself is what prevents judgment from being exercised when it would matter most.

This is why organizations feel trapped by their own plans. They are not unable to change because they lack intelligence or intent. They are unable to change because portfolio logic has converted choice into obligation. What began as strategy becomes identity. What began as an initiative becomes a commitment that cannot be questioned without threatening coherence.

That is also why it is so difficult to build regenerative systems inside project-driven organizations. Regeneration requires learning that can interrupt motion. It requires reversibility after approval, not just before it. It requires protected pause capacity, not just early diligence. It requires a system that can stop without treating stopping as failure.

Portfolios can support that. Most do not, because most were designed to do something else.

Why This Matters for Regeneration

Regenerative systems treat portfolios as conditional commitments, not declarations of inevitability. They preserve reversibility beyond initial approval. They protect the ability to stop work without reputational penalty once learning emerges. They treat investment as provisional and revisable, not as moral obligation.

In such systems, portfolios do not replace judgment. They sustain it. They remain a space where the future can be revised, not merely tracked.

This chapter is not an argument against portfolios. It is an argument against treating portfolio commitment as final. When stopping becomes indistinguishable from failure, regeneration is structurally impossible. The organization can talk about ethics, purpose, and sustainability while continuing to run a portfolio system that converts learning into risk management and doubt into disruption.

The chapters that follow examine what it would take to redesign portfolio logic so that judgment, pause, and refusal remain available even after work has begun. Until then, portfolios will continue to decide futures long before people experience the freedom to choose them.

Chapter 9
Assurance as Safety

Most organizations believe they are good at managing risk. They have registers, controls, dashboards, and review cycles. Risk is identified, assessed, categorized, and tracked. Mitigations are assigned. Residual exposure is accepted. Oversight bodies receive regular updates. When questioned, leaders can point to evidence that risk was raised, documented, and managed.

This belief is sincere. It is also often wrong.

What many organizations call risk management is not a mechanism for preventing harm. It is a mechanism for translating unease into acceptability. It converts live discomfort into procedural comfort. It allows systems to continue moving while maintaining the appearance of responsibility.

Risk does not stop decisions. It makes them defensible.

Across sectors and industries, the same pattern appears with remarkable consistency. A concern is raised. It is reframed as a risk. The risk is logged. Mitigations are identified. Residual exposure is accepted. The dashboard turns green. Once this pattern completes, continuation no longer feels reckless. It feels responsible.

Once a risk is logged, it becomes acceptable by default unless it threatens delivery.

Cost to schedule is explicit, modeled, and argued. Cost to people or ecosystems is abstract, deferred, and externalized.

The original concern has not been resolved. It has been transformed. What began as a question about whether to proceed has become a question about how to proceed safely. The moral weight of the decision is redistributed across process, documentation, and oversight. The system can now move forward with confidence.

This transformation is rarely experienced as cynical. It feels like professionalism. The organization is doing what it is supposed to do. It is acknowledging uncertainty, tracking exposure, and acting within defined tolerances. Everyone involved can point to artifacts that demonstrate diligence.

What those artifacts rarely show is whether the decision itself still makes sense.

Earlier in this book, we saw how a recommendation to stop quietly becomes a plan to monitor. The language shifts subtly. A condition that requires resolution becomes a scenario to manage. A pause becomes enhanced oversight. The word *stop* disappears, replaced by *monitor, mitigate,* and *review.*

No one asks for this change explicitly. It emerges through questions about schedule impact, delivery confidence, and reputational risk. Each edit makes the concern easier to carry forward without interruption. Each one feels reasonable on its own. By the time the issue reaches formal review, the transformation is complete.

The risk is now framed in language that fits the organization's assurance machinery. It can be categorized, assigned, and tracked. It no longer threatens momentum. It no longer requires refusal. What has changed is not the underlying condition. What has changed is the system's relationship to it.

Once a risk is logged, it becomes acceptable by default unless it threatens delivery.
This is the quiet moral inversion at the heart of modern assurance.

Risk registers are not neutral records of uncertainty. They are translation devices. They convert complex, qualitative concerns into standardized fields that can move through governance processes. Probability is estimated. Impact is scored. Mitigation is proposed. Ownership is assigned. Review cadence is set. Each step simplifies reality in a way that allows work to continue.

This simplification is necessary to some degree. Organizations cannot operate if every concern remains open-ended and unresolved. But when the register becomes the primary place where concern is expressed, something important is lost. The question shifts from "should we proceed?" to "is this risk acceptable?"

Acceptability becomes the dominant lens

Acceptable risk does not mean risk has been eliminated. It means the organization has decided it is willing to live with the consequences. That decision is rarely made explicitly. It is inferred through thresholds, tolerances, and color codes.

Green does not mean safe. It means permitted. I've signed off on green checklists, scorecards, and dashboards like this, relieved by their clarity and uneasy about what they were not showing me.

Dashboards reinforce this logic. They present risk as a set of indicators that can be monitored over time. Trends are tracked. Variance is visualized. Leaders are reassured that nothing unexpected is happening because what is happening is being measured.

This creates a powerful illusion of control. The organization feels informed. Leadership feels engaged. Oversight feels active. Decisions feel grounded in data. The system appears to be learning, because numbers are changing and reports are being updated.

What dashboards rarely show is whether the decision itself should be revisited. They show movement, not meaning. They show compliance with process, not confrontation with consequence. As long as indicators remain within tolerance, the system treats continuation as validated.

Green does not mean safe.
It means the system can relax.

Residual risk is often treated as a technical concept. It is described as the exposure that remains after mitigation has been applied. In theory, accepting residual risk is a conscious act. It reflects the organization's willingness to proceed despite uncertainty.

In practice, residual risk often functions as permission. Once a risk is described as residual, it is no longer expected to block progress. It is something to be lived with rather than something to be resolved. The organization acknowledges its existence while insulating the decision from further challenge.

Residual risk accepted.

Those words appear in countless reports and postmortems. They are meant to signal realism and maturity. They often signal something else entirely. They signal that the system has decided not to stop.

This is where assurance reveals its real function. Assurance here does not mean safety. It means the ability to show, after the fact, that the organization behaved according to its own rules.

Assurance frameworks complete the transformation. They provide confirmation that processes were followed, reviews were conducted, and controls were in place. When outcomes fail, assurance documentation becomes evidence that the organization acted responsibly within its own logic.

This matters enormously in moments of scrutiny. Investigations ask whether risks were identified, whether mitigation plans existed, whether escalation occurred. If the answers are yes, the system is often judged diligent, even if the outcome was harmful.

The question of whether the decision itself should have been different recedes. Responsibility shifts from judgment to traceability. As long as the paper trail is intact, the organization can demonstrate that it did what it was supposed to do.

This is not corruption. It is the system protecting itself.

Here is the line that separates management from pre-justification.
If your risk process cannot produce a real stop, you are not managing risk.
You are producing alibis in advance.

A risk process that only ever leads to mitigation and monitoring is not a safeguard. It is a translation mechanism that allows the organization to proceed while feeling responsible. This is why so many systems are surprised by failures they "saw coming."

They did see them coming. They tracked them. They logged them. They monitored them. What they did not do was allow those risks to interrupt motion.

Assurance feels comforting because it replaces moral uncertainty with procedural certainty. People know what to do. They know how to raise concerns. They know how risks will be handled. They know that following the process will protect them professionally.

This comfort is seductive. It allows conscientious people to participate in decisions they privately doubt while telling themselves they have done their duty. The concern was raised. The risk was logged. The mitigation was proposed. The rest is out of their hands.

This is how systems recruit good intentions into harmful trajectories. Not through coercion. Through reassurance.

Once a dashboard turns green, the system relaxes. Attention shifts elsewhere. Energy is reallocated. New priorities emerge. The decision fades into the background as execution proceeds.

The cost does not disappear. It is simply displaced.

Teams absorb it. Communities absorb it. Ecosystems absorb it. Trust absorbs it.
Assurance absorbs none of it. It only records that the transfer was procedurally correct.

By the time the cost becomes visible, it is often described as unfortunate, unintended, or unforeseeable. The documentation suggests otherwise. The system knew. The system tracked. The system managed.

What the system did not do was stop.

Where in your own system has "residual risk accepted" become the moment everyone relaxes instead of the moment someone asks whether the decision still makes sense?

Regenerative systems do not treat assurance as safety. They treat assurance as information. They design risk processes that can escalate to refusal. They treat logging a risk as the beginning of judgment, not its end. They understand that some forms of uncertainty cannot be mitigated without changing direction.

In such systems, green does not mean go. It means pause, revisit, and decide again.

This chapter is not an argument against risk management. It is an argument against confusing traceability with responsibility. When assurance replaces judgment, systems become very good at proving they acted responsibly while continuing to produce harm.

The chapters that follow examine what happens when refusal is structurally unavailable, and why courage is irrelevant when the system makes saying no professionally suicidal.

Until then, risk will continue to function as a permission slip rather than a safeguard, and assurance will continue to launder unease into defensibility.

Chapter 10

Where Refusal Disappears

Many organizations have designed ways for concerns to be raised without allowing work to be interrupted, and they have done so deliberately, with the language of openness, learning, and responsibility. Feedback loops, escalation paths, and formal opportunities to raise issues exist to surface information while preserving momentum, ensuring that dissent can be expressed without threatening delivery. From the outside, these designs suggest that refusal is possible, even welcome, because voice is visible and process appears intact.

What these systems preserve is the ability to speak, not the ability to stop.

Concerns are invited, but only within boundaries that keep work moving. Questions are encouraged, but only so long as they can be resolved into alignment. Escalation is available, but it functions primarily as a translation mechanism, reshaping discomfort into forms that can be logged, monitored, and managed without requiring interruption. What disappears in this design is not disagreement, but the capacity to stop.

Refusal is different from dissent. Dissent allows work to continue after being heard. Refusal interrupts work by insisting that the decision itself cannot be carried forward without redesign, delay, or loss. It requires the system to pause in ways that threaten schedules, commitments, and identity. Systems built to protect continuity experience that interruption not as judgment, but as disruption.

This is why refusal has largely disappeared from modern organizational life. It has not been outlawed, discouraged, or condemned outright. It has been designed out, replaced by forms of voice that feel participatory while ensuring that momentum remains intact. What survives is the appearance of challenge. What vanishes is the ability to say no in a way that changes what happens next.

Dissent Is Permitted. Refusal Is Not.

Most organizations are comfortable with dissent because dissent does not require the system to change its course. People can disagree in meetings, surface alternative views, and challenge assumptions as long as the discussion eventually resolves into alignment. Dissent improves the quality of the decision while preserving its execution, which makes it safe, even valuable, in systems optimized for continuity.

Refusal operates differently. Refusal does not argue for a better way to proceed; it questions whether proceeding is legitimate at all. It asks the organization to pause, revisit assumptions, or accept loss. Where dissent fits inside decision processes, refusal challenges the existence of the decision itself.

Systems built to protect momentum experience that challenge as destabilizing.

As a result, refusal is rarely confronted directly. Instead, it is translated. What might have been refusal is reframed as resistance, misalignment, or lack of commercial awareness. The language shifts, but the effect is consistent. The system absorbs the signal while neutralizing its capacity to interrupt motion.

The surest sign refusal has been translated is when the story shifts from *"should we do this?"* to *"why can't they get on board?"*

Over time, this translation becomes habitual. People learn which kinds of challenge are welcomed and which ones quietly mark them as difficult. The organization preserves the appearance of openness while eliminating the possibility of stoppage.

The Contractual Plane

One place refusal disappears is in contract design.

Termination clauses, penalties, minimum commitments, and performance covenants make stopping materially costly. These costs are explicit, modeled, and negotiated in advance. They appear in financial forecasts and risk summaries. They are discussed seriously, because they threaten delivery and reputation.

The costs of harm are not treated the same way.

Environmental damage, community impact, moral injury, and long-term trust erosion are abstract, deferred, and externalized. They rarely carry immediate price tags, and when they do, those costs are often socialized rather than owned. When refusal would trigger contractual penalties while continuation merely increases externalized harm, the system's preference is already set.

Refusal has been priced out.

The penalties are modeled in detail; the consequences to people and ecosystems are treated like residual risk—acknowledged, but not allowed to interfere.

This is not a failure of values. It is the predictable outcome of treating financial exposure as real and human or ecological exposure as contingent. Once refusal carries a visible cost that continuation does not, the organization has effectively decided in advance.

Reputation and Procedure

Refusal disappears first through reputation, and then through procedure. The two reinforce each other so reliably that they often feel like a single, neutral system at work rather than a coordinated pattern.

People who refuse are rarely described as unethical or uncooperative. They are described as impractical, not strategic, not commercial, or difficult to work with. These labels sound observational rather than judgmental, but they travel quickly. They shape who is invited into future conversations, who is trusted with complex work, and who is quietly excluded from decisions that matter.

Over time, the organization learns who will find a way to proceed and who will insist on stopping. Those who refuse are not usually fired. They are sidelined. Their careers stall. Their influence diminishes. They become examples, not leaders.

You know this person. The one everyone describes as *"brilliant, but..."*
The *"but"* is always that they tried to stop something the system had already decided to do.

The system does not need to punish refusal overtly. It simply stops rewarding it, and the lesson is learned without being spoken.

Procedure then completes what reputation begins.

Escalation pathways remain available, but they rarely lead to interruption. Concerns are noted, risks are logged, mitigations are proposed, and reviews are scheduled. The language of seriousness is preserved even as the outcome remains unchanged. What looks like responsiveness functions as absorption.

Escalation becomes theater.

It allows people to say they raised the issue without forcing the system to act on it. The concern moves upward, but it does not change direction. At each level, it is reframed in language that makes continuation easier to justify and harder to interrupt. What began as a challenge to proceed becomes information about how to proceed safely.

By the time the issue reaches formal authority, it no longer arrives as refusal. It arrives as something manageable.

Noted. Mitigated. Proceed.

This is not a failure of governance. It is governance operating after the decision has already been made, using process to stabilize what reputation has already sorted. Together, reputation and procedure ensure that refusal disappears without ever needing to be prohibited. The system remains orderly. Momentum is preserved. And everyone involved can point to evidence that the issue was handled correctly.

What vanishes is the ability to stop. Watching this happen in real time was one of the moments that finally convinced me this was not a culture problem.

Authority Without Refusal

Earlier in this book, we saw how authority increasingly arrives after choice has collapsed. Boards approve what they cannot stop. Executives manage consequences they did not meaningfully shape. That same dynamic explains why refusal disappears.

Authority without the ability to refuse is not authority. It is endorsement under constraint.

At that point, the board is not governing; it is ratifying a portfolio it can no longer unwind.

When leaders are asked to approve decisions already embedded in portfolios, contracts, and commitments, saying no is no longer a decision. It is a disruption of identity. The cost is not only financial. It is reputational, relational, and political.

This is why even senior leaders hesitate to refuse. Not because they lack courage, but because refusal has been made structurally implausible.

Failed Refusals

The moments where refusal might have occurred are visible throughout this book.

The document that originally said stop and later said monitor.
The meeting that ended early because late insight no

longer fit.

The board member who asked what it would take to stop and received an answer about social impossibility rather than technical constraint.

These are not examples of people failing to speak.

They are examples of refusal being neutralized.

The system absorbed the concern by changing its form. What was raised as a question about whether the work should continue was reshaped into language that made continuation possible. The phrasing softened. The scope narrowed. The implication was reframed as a manageable condition rather than a decision point. Responsibility dispersed across committees, registers, and review cycles, until no single moment required a stop.

What had originally been a refusal did not disappear. It was translated. It became a risk to be monitored, a dependency to be managed, an assumption to be revisited later. Each translation preserved momentum while reducing the concern's ability to interrupt. By the time the issue reached formal authority, it no longer arrived as a challenge to proceed. It arrived as information about how to proceed safely.

Refusal did not fail because it was unreasonable or ill-timed. It failed because the structure could not hold it. The system was designed to metabolize exactly this kind of discomfort, converting it into forms that fit existing processes and timelines. Once that conversion was complete, continuation was no longer a choice. It was simply what came next.

Courage Without Permission

Organizations often respond to this dynamic by calling for courage. They ask leaders to be bolder, to speak truth to power, to hold the line. These calls sound noble. They are also a distraction.

Courage without permission is a trap.

When refusal reliably damages careers, courage becomes a personal sacrifice rather than a system function. The organization preserves its structure by transferring the cost of integrity onto individuals.

This is not leadership development. It is displacement.

If refusing a decision reliably ends a career, the organization does not have leaders. It has high-status operators who are rewarded for making the system work as designed.

Why This Matters for Regeneration

Regenerative systems do not depend on courage to produce refusal. They design refusal into the system.

They create roles that can say no without penalty. They structure contracts that do not price refusal out. They design escalation pathways that can interrupt motion rather than merely record concern. They treat stopping as competence rather than as failure of planning.

In such systems, refusal is not heroic. It is normal.

If your system still relies on individual heroism for refusal to occur, you have chosen design avoidance.

This chapter is not an argument for braver leaders. It is an argument for making refusal structurally valid and professionally survivable. Without that, regeneration remains rhetorical. Systems will continue to praise values while eliminating the ability to act on them.

If someone in your organization exercised genuine refusal tomorrow, would they still be promotable a year from now?

The chapter that follows names the cost of making refusal real, and why systems unwilling to give up speed, optionality, and convenience will continue to ask others to absorb the consequences on their behalf.

Chapter 11

The Real Cost of Regeneration

Regeneration is often described as ambition. It is framed as a higher form of performance, a more enlightened way of operating, or a competitive advantage waiting to be unlocked. In this telling, regeneration can be layered onto existing systems without fundamentally changing how those systems decide, commit, and protect themselves. It promises progress without sacrifice and improvement without loss.

That promise is appealing. It is also false.

Regeneration is not additive. It does not expand what organizations can do. It narrows what they are willing to do, when they are willing to do it, and how much harm they are prepared to externalize in the process. The real cost of regeneration is not effort or intent. It is power. In my own work, that cost has shown up as decisions I no longer get kudos for making.

Speed

Regenerative systems give up speed, not because slowness is virtuous, but because they understand what speed does to judgment. Earlier in this book, we saw how speed collapses time, hardens commitment, and makes stopping professionally implausible. Once continuation becomes the only realistic option, harm is no longer prevented. It is merely managed, deferred, or displaced.

The meeting that ended early earlier in this book ended because alignment suppressed late insight. In a regenerative system, that same meeting would end without a decision, and with explicit acceptance of a missed window. The cost would be visible. The pause would be intentional. No one would rush to translate hesitation into momentum.

Choosing regeneration means refusing to compress judgment into delivery timelines. It means accepting missed opportunities rather than forcing decisions before their consequences can be seen. It means tolerating uncertainty instead of resolving it prematurely through motion.

If you are currently rewarded for decisiveness under pressure, this will make you look slower, less certain, and less promotable.

Inside the organization, this feels like inefficiency. Outside, it looks like hesitation. In reality, it is restraint.

Optionality

Regenerative systems give up optionality. Modern organizations are designed to keep options open, not to choose decisively. Portfolios are structured to preserve flexibility, pipelines are maintained to avoid hard tradeoffs, and initiatives are kept alive long past their usefulness so that nothing has to be definitively stopped.

Earlier chapters showed how portfolios convert intent into obligation and treat stopping as failure. The portfolio you saw earlier that locked harm in place would, under regenerative conditions, have been forced to trigger a stop at the moment the risk memo first said "stop," rather than translating it into monitoring.

Regeneration requires committing to fewer things, more conditionally, and with explicit acknowledgment of what will be lost if those commitments prove wrong. It means allowing work to end without being replaced by something equally consuming. It means choosing depth over breadth, and consequence over coverage.

This is not strategic elegance.

It is constraint.

Growth Trajectories

Regenerative systems give up guaranteed growth trajectories. In many organizations, growth is not treated as a choice but as a moral expectation. Expansion, scale, and continuation are equated with integrity, while contraction is treated as weakness or failure. Once growth becomes non-negotiable, decisions that increase harm become inevitable.

Regeneration breaks that equation. It accepts volatility in outcomes rather than locking in harm to preserve predictability. It allows revenue, output, or market presence to fluctuate rather than committing to trajectories that require continuous extraction. It treats stability of impact as more important than stability of metrics.

If your bonus, legitimacy, or authority depends on smooth upward curves, this will threaten all three.

This is not anti-growth. It is anti-inevitability.

Decision Rights

Regenerative systems give up centralized decision rights exercised late. Earlier in this book, we saw how authority increasingly arrives after choice has collapsed, leaving boards to approve what they cannot stop and executives to manage consequences they did not meaningfully shape.

The board that ratified a portfolio it could not unwind would lose the comfort of late approval entirely. Authority would have to arrive before commitments harden, or not at all.

Regeneration requires moving authority earlier rather than higher. It means granting real decision rights before commitments lock in, even when that slows throughput and complicates coordination. It means allowing refusal to occur upstream rather than absorbing it downstream.

What is relinquished here is not control itself, but the illusion that control can be exercised after the fact.

Convenience

Regenerative systems give up convenience. Dashboards, KPIs, assurance frameworks, and reporting structures provide comfort by compressing complexity into formats that can move through governance without friction. They allow leaders to feel informed and responsible without being exposed to the full texture of consequence.

Earlier chapters showed how these tools replace judgment with traceability. Regeneration requires tolerating discomfort instead. It means allowing unresolved tension to remain visible rather than smoothing it away. It means designing processes that surface difficulty rather than anesthetize it.

This is not better information design.

It is refusal to numb.

Plausible Deniability

Regenerative systems give up plausible deniability. Much of modern organizational life is structured so that no one ever has to fully own the conditions that produced harm. Risk registers, assurance reports, escalation records, and postmortems distribute responsibility across process and time. When failure occurs, the system can demonstrate that it behaved according to its own rules.

This isn't an aberration. It is insulation.

Regeneration removes that insulation. It reduces the number of places consequences can be sent that cannot say no. It forces organizations to confront outcomes without the buffer of procedure.

If you have built a career on being the safe pair of hands inside extractive structures, this removes your cover.

Why This Cannot Be Softened

None of these losses can be reframed as gains without collapsing the argument of this book. If speed is preserved, judgment will be compressed. If optionality is preserved, stopping will remain taboo. If growth remains non-negotiable, harm will be locked in. If authority arrives late, refusal will remain impossible. If convenience is prioritized, assurance will continue to replace responsibility. If deniability remains intact, regeneration will remain rhetorical.

If you keep speed, optionality, non-negotiable growth, late authority, convenience, and deniability largely intact, you are not practicing regeneration. You are running an extractive system with better language. This is not a matter of leadership mindset. It is a matter of design.

Why This Cannot Be Softened

None of these losses can be reframed as gains without collapsing the argument of this book. If speed is preserved, judgment will continue to be compressed. If optionality is preserved, stopping will remain taboo. If growth remains non-negotiable, harm will continue to be locked in under the language of success. If authority arrives late, refusal will remain structurally impossible. If convenience is prioritized, assurance will continue to replace responsibility. If deniability remains intact, regeneration will remain rhetorical.

These are not philosophical tensions. They are design facts.

You have already seen the rooms where these facts play out.

The meeting that ended early because late insight no longer fit ended that way because speed was treated as non-negotiable. In a regenerative system, that same meeting would end without a decision, and with explicit acceptance of the cost of delay. The window would close. The opportunity would be missed. And no one would rush to translate hesitation into momentum to protect their credibility.

The portfolio that converted intent into obligation and locked harm in place did so because optionality was treated as virtue. In a regenerative system, that portfolio would have been forced to trigger a stop at the moment the risk memo first said *stop*, not weeks later when monitoring replaced judgment. Capital would be retracted. Plans would unravel. Careers attached to that initiative would feel exposed.

The board that ratified what it could not unwind did so because authority arrived after commitment hardened. In a regenerative system, that board would lose the comfort of late approval entirely. Authority would arrive before portfolios locked in, or not at all. Some decisions would never reach the board because they would be constrained earlier, where refusal was still possible.

This is where the cost becomes personal.

If you are currently rewarded for decisiveness under pressure, this will make you look indecisive.
If your status, compensation, or legitimacy depend on smooth upward curves, this will threaten all three.
If you have built a career on being the safe pair of hands who keeps things moving inside extractive structures, regeneration will remove the cover that made that role comfortable.

This is not organizational sacrifice. It is individual exposure.

Regeneration does not ask the system, in the abstract, to give things up. It asks specific people to relinquish advantages they currently enjoy: speed without consequence, growth without interruption, authority without refusal, and responsibility without proximity to harm.

That is why regeneration cannot be piloted safely. It cannot be trialed at the edges while the center remains untouched. It cannot be delegated to sustainability teams or innovation labs without changing how portfolios commit, how boards approve, and how refusal is priced.

If speed, optionality, non-negotiable growth, late authority, convenience, and deniability remain largely intact, you are not on a regenerative journey. You are running an extractive system with upgraded language.

This is not a matter of leadership mindset. It is a matter of design.

Some organizations will choose not to make this trade. They will adopt regenerative vocabulary while preserving the same commitment engines, the same assurance rituals, and the same career incentives. They will replace leaders when harm becomes visible rather than redesigning the structures that made harm inevitable.

They should not be allowed to call that regeneration.

At this point, the reader is no longer dealing with theory. You have seen the mechanisms. You have recognized the rooms. You know where judgment is lost, where refusal disappears, and where harm is displaced.

The remaining question is not whether regeneration is desirable.

It is whether you are willing to accept the limits it demands, or whether you will continue to ask others to absorb the consequences of refusing them.

The chapter that follows does not offer a framework or a path forward. It describes what organizations look like when they actually redesign for judgment rather than performance, and what changes when pause, refusal, and restraint are treated not as leadership failures, but as properties of the system itself.

Chapter 12
What It Looks Like When Judgment Wins

The final illusion to fall is the most comfortable one.

After speed has been questioned, refusal reclaimed, and cost made explicit, many readers will still hold onto a familiar hope: that what is missing is a better framework. A clearer method. A smarter governance model. A way to operationalize judgment without disturbing the deeper structures that make judgment inconvenient.

That hope is understandable.

It is also misplaced.

Judgment does not fail in modern organizations because the right tools have not been found. It fails because the system is designed to move past it. No framework can compensate for that design. What matters is not the sophistication of the method, but the conditions under which judgment is allowed to survive.

This chapter does not describe a solution. It describes a difference.

The Same Rooms, Behaving Differently

Earlier in this book, you encountered a meeting that ended early. It ended not because clarity had been achieved, but because late insight no longer fit the momentum already in motion. Alignment resolved uncertainty by closing the conversation.

In a system where judgment wins, that same meeting ends early for a different reason. It ends because a late concern triggers a designed pause, not an awkward silence. The group recognizes that the decision has crossed from deliberation into commitment prematurely. No one rushes to translate discomfort into reassurance. The meeting ends without a decision, and the cost of delay is named explicitly rather than disguised as inefficiency.

The window closes. The opportunity may be lost. That loss is accepted as the price of not locking in harm.

In most organizations, the person who called that pause would quietly lose influence. Here, they gain it. Their willingness to stop becomes evidence of seniority, not a reason to question their readiness.

Earlier, you saw a risk memo whose language softened from *stop* to *monitor* as it moved upward. The memo survived, but its capacity to interrupt did not. Assurance replaced judgment.

In a system where judgment wins, that same memo does not need to be heroic. It does not rely on forceful language or personal credibility. It enters a process that is designed to treat *stop* as a legitimate outcome, not as a failure of planning. The memo does not get translated into monitoring because monitoring is not the default response to discomfort. The question it raises is allowed to remain unresolved long enough to matter.

The work pauses. Capital is not yet withdrawn, but neither is it treated as obligated. The system absorbs uncertainty rather than exporting it.

In most systems, the author would be praised for pragmatism when they soften the language. Here, they would be asked why they retreated, and whether they still stand behind the concern.

Earlier, you saw a board approve a decision it could not stop. Authority arrived after commitment had hardened, leaving oversight to ratify inevitability.

In a system where judgment wins, that board never sees that decision in its hardened form. The portfolio that would have locked it in has already been constrained upstream. Authority arrives earlier, where refusal is still plausible. The board's work shifts from endorsing continuity to defining limits. Fewer decisions reach the room, not because they are smaller, but because they have already been bounded by design.

The room feels quieter. Less busy. More consequential.

The difference is not in who sits around the table. It is in what the table is allowed to do.

One Day in the Life of a Decision

Imagine a decision that, in most organizations, would follow the familiar path from intent to obligation: a major program, acquisition, or expansion. In the world you know, it would enter a pipeline, join a portfolio, accumulate commitments, and eventually reach a point where stopping became impractical, even when doubts remained.

In a system where judgment wins, the same decision moves differently.

It begins like many others, as an idea and a narrative about opportunity. But before it becomes a project, it is asked a different set of questions. Not only "What is the upside?" but "Where could this realistically be stopped, and by whom?" Kill switches are not an afterthought. They are part of the initial design.

Funding is released in stages that preserve reversibility. Each stage carries explicit conditions under which continuation is not merely reviewed, but expected to be refused if certain signals appear. Those signals are not limited to financial variance. They include indicators of harm, overload, and judgment being compressed.

As the work begins, teams know that bringing forward uncomfortable information will not simply result in more mitigation. It may trigger the next pause. Their role is not to make the decision work at any cost, but to keep the decision honest.

A familiar moment arrives. A concern emerges that does not fit cleanly into existing risk categories. It is not catastrophic on its own, but it hints at compounding effects under pressure. In other organizations, naming such a concern would mark the speaker as difficult. Here, it is exactly what the system is designed to surface.

The concern is raised. It is logged, but not immediately translated into something manageable. Instead, the act of logging triggers a pre-agreed pause. The next governance discussion is no longer about confidence to proceed. It is about whether the conditions that justified the decision still exist.

The room gathers. The agenda is shorter than usual. The question is narrower and heavier: not "Are we on track?" but "Do we still believe we should be doing this at all?" Data is reviewed, not to demonstrate control, but to test whether the original assumptions still hold.

No one in the room is neutral. Effort and reputation have already been invested. In most systems, that fact alone would tilt the discussion toward continuation. Here, the bias is named. One person explicitly acknowledges their conflict of interest and steps out of the final call.

The decision is not unanimous. It is also not deferred. The kill switch is pulled. The work stops.

There is no crisis narrative and no search for a scapegoat. There is an explanation: the conditions under which the work was justified no longer exist, and the system is unwilling to trade harm for momentum.

People who worked on the program are not punished. They are recognized for carrying the work honestly to a point where stopping was the most responsible outcome.

From the outside, this looks like caution. From the inside, it feels like coherence.

The difference is not that these people cared more. It is that the structure allowed their care to change what happened next.

How These Differences Are Produced

None of these differences require exceptional people.

They are not the result of better courage, stronger values, or superior leadership development. They emerge from ordinary structures behaving differently under pressure.

Earlier in this book, speed produced a point of no pause where continuation became inevitable. In systems where judgment wins, pause is protected rather than penalized. It cannot be overridden casually, and invoking it does not damage credibility. Speed remains available, but it is no longer treated as a moral good. Moving fast requires justification; waiting does not.

Earlier, refusal required courage without permission. Here, refusal is structurally valid. Contracts do not price it out. Escalation pathways do not translate it away. Roles are designed to carry it without personal sacrifice. Saying no does not end a career, and therefore does not require heroism.

Earlier, portfolios converted intent into obligation. Here, portfolios commit conditionally. Funding is released in ways that preserve reversibility beyond initial approval. Stopping work is treated as competence rather than as waste, and is rewarded accordingly.

Earlier, assurance functioned as alibis in advance. Here, assurance remains, but it does not replace judgment. Dashboards inform decisions rather than closing them. Green indicators do not signal safety; they signal readiness to decide again.

Earlier, authority arrived late and ratified what could not be unwound. Here, authority arrives before commitment, not after. Boards and executives define the conditions under which work may proceed and the conditions under which it must stop.

None of this is dramatic.

That is the point.

Why Frameworks Cannot Do This Work

It is tempting to look at these differences and ask how to codify them.

What framework would ensure protected pause. What governance model would normalize refusal. What maturity assessment would signal readiness.

These questions misunderstand the problem.

Judgment does not fail because it has not been formalized. It fails because formalization is often used to make continuation safer rather than to keep choice alive. Frameworks travel easily. They are adopted selectively. They are implemented without disturbing the incentives that matter most.

A system that depends on exceptional people to override its own momentum is not designed for judgment. It is designed for survival under pressure.

If judgment depends on exceptional people rather than ordinary structure, it will not survive contact with pressure.

No template can change that. At best, it can reveal where the system is unwilling to give up speed, optionality, or deniability. At worst, it becomes another layer of assurance—more evidence that the right questions were asked, even as the same answers are chosen.

How It Feels from the Inside

When judgment wins, the organization becomes less impressive.

Decisions take longer. Opportunities are missed. Growth curves wobble. Narratives are harder to maintain. Some work never begins, and some work ends early without being replaced.

For those whose status, authority, and reward have been built on speed, scale, and smooth narratives, this does not feel like evolution. It feels like loss of power.

For those in the middle, the change feels different. The constant pressure to translate discomfort into motion eases. The need to soften language, to reframe *stop* as *monitor*, to absorb contradictions that cannot be resolved begins to recede. Their work shifts from protecting senior narratives to protecting judgment itself.

For those at the edges—teams, communities, ecosystems—the change is quieter still. Shocks arrive less often and with less force. Harm is not eliminated, but it is less frequently treated as a regrettable surprise. The system becomes more honest about where consequences land and more deliberate about who is asked to carry them.

Over time, something fundamental changes. Responsibility becomes harder to displace. Decisions that matter become easier to see. The organization stops confusing motion with progress.

Judgment does not make the organization kinder.

It makes it accountable.

The Non-Negotiable Line

If judgment depends on exceptional people rather than ordinary structure, it will not survive contact with pressure.

The Audit Question

Where, in your own system, could a decision be paused today without anyone losing credibility, momentum, or career capital?

Chapter 13

The Responsibility of Knowing

This book began by naming an ancient error: when systems fail, we replace people. We change leaders, rotate roles, issue apologies, and announce new commitments, telling ourselves that the problem was judgment, character, or competence rather than design. That error has endured because it is comforting. It allows institutions to preserve their structures while sacrificing those who could no longer carry their consequences, and it allows harm to be treated as deviation rather than as signal.

Everything you have read since then has been an argument against that displacement.

Responsibility is often described as ownership of outcomes, but in practice it has come to mean something narrower and safer: being accountable for delivery within conditions you did not choose, using tools you did not design, toward ends that were already decided. This version of responsibility is compatible with extraction. It allows people to feel ethical while participating in systems that continue to export harm, and it allows organizations to claim integrity without confronting the designs that make harm inevitable.

That is not responsibility.

Responsibility, as this book has used the word, is ownership of design conditions. It is the willingness to see how pressure, power, and consequence move through a system, and to accept that those movements are produced rather than accidental. Once that becomes visible, responsibility changes character. It is no longer about being the best person inside the system. It becomes a question of whether the system itself is acceptable.

Throughout this book, you have seen how replacement functions. When risk materializes, the sponsor changes. When delivery fails, the manager moves on. When harm becomes visible, leadership is refreshed. The system remains. Replacement restores the appearance of control without altering the conditions that made failure likely, satisfying the demand for accountability while preserving the design that displaced judgment in the first place.

If you finish this book and respond by replacing people rather than redesigning systems, you are repeating the ancient error it opened with. Not out of malice, but out of habit.

Some roles, as they are currently designed, are structurally incompatible with regeneration. This is not an accusation. It is a design fact. There are positions whose legitimacy depends on speed that cannot pause, growth that cannot fluctuate, portfolios that cannot unwind, and assurance that cannot refuse. In such roles, acting regeneratively would require relinquishing the very conditions that define success.

This is not a personal failure. It is a structural incompatibility. What is understandable is not automatically defensible. The structure constrains you; it does not absolve you.

Naming that incompatibility matters because it reframes the ethical conversation. The question is no longer whether someone cares enough or tries hard enough, but whether the role they occupy can be exercised responsibly under the constraints it imposes. Some people will leave those roles. Others will stay and continue to operate extractively, even with greater awareness. Neither choice is morally neutral, but both are comprehensible responses to structural pressure. What is no longer acceptable is pretending that regeneration can be practiced inside designs that forbid it.

At some point while reading this book, a line was crossed. You recognized the rooms where *stop* became *monitor*, where the meeting ended early, where the board could not withhold approval. You saw how concerns were softened, how refusal disappeared, and how harm was displaced. From that moment on, what you knew altered what you were responsible for.

You cannot unknow this. Writing this forced me to revisit decisions I would have defended at the time, and to accept that knowing more now does not retroactively fix them.

Continuing to benefit from a design that exports harm is no longer accidental once the mechanism is visible. Remaining inside it becomes a choice rather than an oversight, even when that choice feels constrained or necessary.

This is the quiet burden of knowing.

This book does not promise that regeneration is achievable everywhere, nor does it promise that redesign will be rewarded or that refusal will be welcomed. In many contexts it will not be. What it offers instead is clarity. It also removes the last safe distance between your role and your system's design. You can no longer treat structure as background and responsibility as personal.

By now, the question is no longer whether regeneration is a compelling idea. It is whether you are willing to accept the limits it imposes and the losses it demands in the places where you have influence, not influence as title, but influence as design choice. You may decide that the cost is too high. You may decide that the system you are in cannot be changed from where you stand. You may decide to continue operating as you are, with fewer illusions.

You will be able to tell yourself a coherent story about each of those choices. That coherence does not change what they are.

What is no longer available is the comfort of saying you did not know.

Given what you now see, what are you still asking others to absorb on your behalf?